Demystifying Smart Cities

Practical Perspectives on How Cities Can Leverage the Potential of New Technologies

Anders Lisdorf

Apress®

Demystifying Smart Cities: Practical Perspectives on How Cities Can Leverage the Potential of New Technologies

Anders Lisdorf
Copenhagen, Denmark

ISBN-13 (pbk): 978-1-4842-5376-2   ISBN-13 (electronic): 978-1-4842-5377-9
https://doi.org/10.1007/978-1-4842-5377-9

Copyright © 2020 by Anders Lisdorf

Managing Director, Apress Media LLC: Welmoed Spahr
Acquisitions Editor: Natalie Pao
Development Editor: James Markham
Coordinating Editor: Jessica Vakili

Distributed to the book trade worldwide by Springer Science+Business Media New York, 233 Spring Street, 6th Floor, New York, NY 10013. Phone 1-800-SPRINGER, fax (201) 348-4505, e-mail orders-ny@springer-sbm.com, or visit www.springeronline.com. Apress Media, LLC is a California LLC and the sole member (owner) is Springer Science + Business Media Finance Inc (SSBM Finance Inc). SSBM Finance Inc is a **Delaware** corporation.

For information on translations, please e-mail rights@apress.com, or visit http://www.apress.com/rights-permissions.

Apress titles may be purchased in bulk for academic, corporate, or promotional use. eBook versions and licenses are also available for most titles. For more information, reference our Print and eBook Bulk Sales web page at http://www.apress.com/bulk-sales.

Any source code or other supplementary material referenced by the author in this book is available to readers on GitHub via the book's product page, located at www.apress.com/ 978-1-4842-5376-2. For more detailed information, please visit http://www.apress.com/ source-code.

Printed on acid-free paper

Table of Contents

About the Author

Anders Lisdorf has worked with innovative technologies for more than a decade in many different settings and industries. The last couple of years, he has been responsible for developing the data services of New York City, but previously he has worked as an entrepreneur, taught at the university level, and worked as a consultant. You can find him online and read more on his blog at www.lisdorf.com.

About the Technical Reviewer

Ahmed Bakir is an iOS author, teacher, and entrepreneur. He has worked on over 30 mobile projects, ranging from advising startups to architecting apps for Fortune 500 companies. In 2014, he published his first book, *Beginning iOS Media App Development*, followed by the first edition of *Program the Internet of Things with Swift for iOS* in 2016 and the second edition in 2018. In 2015, he was invited to develop courses and teach iOS development at UCSD Extension. He is currently building cool stuff in Tokyo! You can find him online at `www.devatelier.com`.

CHAPTER 1

Introduction

One of the first musical memories I have is Queen's music video for "Radio Gaga" in which a bleak future city with flying cars and high rises is portrayed. For some odd reason, I ended up seeing the film that provided the background footage, Fritz Lang's visionary 1927 film *Metropolis*, when I was in first grade at the local library. This left a lasting impression on me about the future of life in cities and the possibilities and challenges they would provide.

Whether we think about the flying cars of a bleak future city in Fritz Lang's *Metropolis*, the hidden underground cities of *The Matrix*, or the city planet Coruscant in the *Star Wars* universe, cities have been a major object of focus for the imagination for centuries. Whether dystopian or utopian, fiction generates expectations and an impetus that drives us to develop new solutions that alter our reality. Cities are a fact of life and will be in the foreseeable future, which is why we have to reflect on how we want our future cities to be and how we can realize that. Switching from the dystopian outlooks of *Metropolis*, this book is about turning fiction into fact by understanding the practical details of leveraging technology to make cities more livable, sustainable, resilient, and prosperous. The book is intended for a nontechnical audience ranging from decision makers over civil servants to business people. For those who want to dive into more technical detail, references are provided at the end of the book for each chapter. The introduction will give an overview of the history of urbanization and look toward the future of cities. We will look at what smart cities are, the primary actors, and the primary area in order to build

© Anders Lisdorf 2020
A. Lisdorf, *Demystifying Smart Cities*, https://doi.org/10.1007/978-1-4842-5377-9_1

a foundation for understanding the different parts of the puzzle and how they fit into the larger context. At the end is a brief outline of the book.

The history and future of cities

Human civilization is inextricably tied to cities. The very term civilization comes from the Latin "civilis" meaning everything related to being a citizen (also from Latin "civis"). This connection is however not just a linguistic artifact of Western culture.

When civilizations began appearing around 3500–3000 BC, in what is called the Fertile Crescent in present-day Middle East, they were all based and grew from cities. The original format well known through millennia was that of the city-state. One of the very first documented city-states is Uruk in ancient Mesopotamia. Other city-states appeared in the same area and spread to Egypt and then the wider Mediterranean.

Although not historically related, similar patterns of urbanization and empire-building were found through the following millennia in China, Mesoamerica (the Maya), and South America (pre-Inca and Inca) and about a thousand years ago in Western Africa. It is as if a wildfire spread through human culture across the globe fueled by urbanization, because on the scale of human development, 5000 years is only a short period of time.

From the very beginning, cities have been dependent on technologies to sustain life and produce ever more sophisticated tools and technologies. The Roman cities would never have been able to grow to the size they did without the aqueducts leading water into all corners of the city. The Egyptians would never have been able to build their marvelous temples and pyramids without their ramps and maps. It is as if the city creates and is created by technologies in an ever-ascending reinforcement loop.

Historically, cities were the exception, with hunter/gatherers as the norm, but today urbanization is a fact of life that very few humans are not affected by. The United Nations released a report on the state of the world's cities in 2011 where they assessed that still in 1950 about 30% of the earth's population was residing in cities, whereas now more than half live in cities, a number expected to reach 80% by 2050.

The British physicist Geoffrey West has even suggested that we call the present time the *Urbanocene* period. This period started after the industrial revolution, which significantly sped up the expansion of cities. He observes: "The future of humanity and long term sustainability of the planet are inextricably linked to the fate of our cities."

We should therefore start preparing for life in cities. But what exactly is so different about cities and what makes life there better? With cities come more opportunities and wealth for its citizens even if this wealth is not evenly distributed. The selection of products, restaurants, entertainment, income, and job opportunities grow with size. The crucial observation demonstrated by the West is that it does not just grow linearly, that is, if you double the number of people, you assume you'd double the number of different types of restaurants, for example. It scales superlinearly with 15% more than would be expected from linear growth. It is simply more exciting to live in cities, and it keeps getting better as it grows. Unfortunately, bad things such as crime, income inequality, disease, and pollution also scale in the same way.

With increases in size also comes an increased need for infrastructure. This is where it gets interesting, for this property does not scale superlinearly, but rather sublineally. This means that whereas average income increases more than expected from a linear growth model, the costs and needs of roads, pipes, and telephony grow less than would be expected from a linear growth model. Even more strangely, this is 15% less than linear growth, which means that when a city is doubled, we only have to spend 85% more on building and maintaining roads, not 100%.

It seems that there is no turning back from the city as the dominant framework in which we will live our lives in the future. Whether we will ever turn the face of our planet into a planet-wide urban cover like the fabled city planet of Coruscant from the *Star Wars* movies may be more doubtful, but the future of humanity depends on cities as the framework in which we need to tackle the most important challenges such as pollution, climate change, disease, and crime, but they also provide the possibility to create new ideas, innovation, and use of technology.

We therefore need to reflect on how we develop cities. This is of course not a new thing, and we have been thinking about this and doing it for centuries. The famous French modernist architect and city planner, Le Corbusier, wrote an interesting book, *The City of To-Morrow and Its Planning*, in the start of the previous century in which he summed up two basic approaches to developing the city: "Man walks in a straight line because he has a goal and knows where he is going (..) the pack-donkey meanders along, meditates a little in his scatter brained and distracted fashion, he zigzags in order to avoid larger stones, or to ease the climb, or to gain shade; he takes the line of least resistance."

The pack donkey becomes the image of the irrational unreflected way of city planning known from the medieval towns, urban sprawl, and slums all over the world. If you have ever admired the winding roads of city centers of Paris, Rome, Zurich, or Copenhagen, you would have experienced the particular charm of a city planned by the way of the pack donkey.

Conversely, the way of man with his straight lines and right angles can be seen in the rational Roman grid–based cities that formed the inspiration for many American cities like New York, Minneapolis, and Lima. These have less of the charm but more efficiency and utility and are definitely easier to find your way in.

While Le Corbusier focused on the physical infrastructure of cities, there is no reason why we cannot generalize the insights to infrastructure in general and technology infrastructure in particular. smart city technology is just another type of infrastructure.

Unfortunately, today most smart city infrastructure is being developed according to the way of the pack donkey in a scatterbrained and distracted fashion with ad hoc implementations following the path of least resistance. Only rarely are there any grand plans or visions in place to guide the technological infrastructure of the city. Most development is done through scattered pilots, grants, and ad hoc partnerships, inspired by political winds that blew favorably for one particular solution regardless of its merits to the city and its residents.

Le Corbusier had his native Paris in mind and admired the clarity with which Louis XIV built a whole new city of Versailles according to rational principles in order to get away from the Parisian medieval city's chaos. This is a radical way of applying the way of man and will not work in most situations. Fortunately for us and past and present tourists who visit Paris, he also instructed his architect Haussmann to come up with a plan to clean up Paris. This was done by carving out massive boulevards through the medieval center.

Often when we see technology being used at scale in cities, it is more in the fashion of Versailles, a greenfield operation, rather than Haussmann's rational incisions into the heart of the Parisian life. After all, it takes courage and leadership to start to demolish buildings in order to build rational new infrastructure. We probably need both approaches, but we definitely need to start thinking about how technology can help solve the challenges and take advantage of the opportunities in our cities.

This book is about the practical application of technology in order to make our cities more resilient, sustainable, and livable, so that we can approach the middle of the century with a clear conscience and optimism for the future of humanity. Today the use and application of technology has not been sufficiently adopted in our cities. This book is a guide to how we can change that.

The Smart City landscape

The concept of a smart city is not a self-explanatory one. Smart city projects are frequently airy visions fueled by vendor marketing. Mega vendors like IBM, GE, Siemens, Citrix, Samsung, and Hitachi have been banging the drums for a decade, but while their ideas are visionary, there is a huge gap between the ideas and the realization of them.

Some may have heard of futuristic cities like Songdo in South Korea or Masdar in Abu Dhabi. They were envisioned as the smart cities of the future. However, they appear more like greenfield exhibits similar to Versailles than the real-life pulsating cities most people live in and want to live in. They have not been successful in much else than showcasing technology and vendors. Anything we may learn would also be difficult to apply because people live in cities that already exist. It is the exception that we will build a city from scratch.

Reading the literature on smart cities will also baffle most. Some are airy in different more philosophical ways. Consider this quote from the excellent book *The City of Tomorrow: Sensors, Networks, Hackers, and the Future of Urban Life*: "Optimization inflected with humanization means neither metropolitan-scale computers nor a network-enabled wild west. It is the convergence of bits and atoms: systems and citizens." It is hard to decode what it actually means and even more so how this is practically applicable in any real-world sense. How will we make cities, the earth, and humanity better given this insight?

Others are more practical but often end up being a disorganized list of interesting insights and projects from across the world. This is great for inspiration, but little will be learned in terms of generalizable and practically applicable insights. There seems to be no book on the fundamentals and practical application of smart city technology to create more livable, resilient, and prosperous cities.

This book aims to demystify this amorphous concept of the smart city and its implications. In order to do this, we should at least start with some sort of understanding of what we mean by the concept smart city.

To get an idea, let us look at a definition that at least has the virtue of being created by a standardization organization, namely, the International Telecommunication Union (ITU):

"A smart sustainable city is an innovative city that uses information and communication technologies (ICTs) and other means to improve quality of life, efficiency of urban operation and services, and competitiveness, while ensuring that it meets the needs of present and future generations with respect to economic, social and environmental aspects."

This gives us a good idea about what we want to talk about but is also a bit vague. What, for example, does it precisely mean that a city is innovative? Can a city not be a smart city if it copies all the best solutions from other cities? Similarly, it is difficult to validate whether the needs of future generations are really met. Strictly speaking, we would have to wait generations in order to find out if a city is indeed a smart city.

Rather than getting lost on definitional details, let us focus on what seems to be the core of the smart city. We want to understand how technology can help a city deal with challenges and provide opportunities for its residents so as to make it a more sustainable, resilient, and livable city.

Understanding the smart city is about understanding technology as the crucial component in softening stresses and shocks like disease, crime, and disasters and improving opportunities like employment, choice, and innovation. All of these themes are already being pursued by standard political means such as legislation and taxation and having hospitals and fire and police stations. The crucial part about the smart city is how technology can add to these existing ways a city pursues its goals.

Actors in the Smart City

In order to understand how smart city solutions are developed, implemented, and maintained in practice, we need to consider the actors in a city. We need to understand the interests and goals of different types of actors that make smart city implementations possible or impossible. Even though the end goal of a functioning city may be the same, the motivations, power, and interests are very different. These groups follow very different logics, and a failure to understand this is a cause of many failures of smart city implementations resulting in an inability to harvest the full potential of technology. Consequently, we will spend some time to get acquainted with the different actors in smart city implementations and understand their particular interests and logic.

Individuals

Individuals are the people living, working, or staying in the city, basically the people who come there for one reason or another. Obviously, these individuals are very different and belong to multiple different ethnic and religious groups, but from a smart city perspective, they are fairly similar. We can distinguish three primary groups of individuals that have a different interest in smart cities.

Residents – Are the individuals residing in the city permanently. They are the ones who have their official address registered in the city and are able to take advantage of the city's offerings like benefits and health care and participate in voting. Since they have their day-to-day life in the city, their primary interests are the functioning of the city's services and infrastructure. They are a primary group to keep happy since they are the ones complaining and, in a democratic context, vote for the city's elected officials. If traffic or pollution is too bad, they will move away, and the city will miss their contributions.

Visitors – This is a group that is often missed from smart city discussions, but many cities like New York, London, and Paris have significant economic incentives to keep tourists happy. Tourists don't need access to social services and health care like residents, but they do need mobility and infrastructure like wifi access points, chargers, and such. Another group of visitors are seasonal workers. Their needs are somewhere in between visitors and residents.

Civic activists – Are naturally a subset of residents, but their behavior is very different, because they are not just more or less passive consumers of city services but actively participate in shaping and producing novel smart city solutions.

Businesses

One of the most important actors are businesses as they drive many of the primary functions of a city. Having businesses operate in a city not only creates jobs in those companies and brings in tax revenue to the city; it also creates demand for other businesses and services. Frequently, smart city initiatives start as engagements with the local business community or are conceived as natural extensions of economic development plans. Sometimes this is done through zoning where special areas are reserved for technology experimentations, and at other times, it is done through the city investing in new infrastructure that can be characterized as smart city initiatives.

Vendors

These are the entities actively engaged in developing, deploying, and maintaining smart city solutions. To some extent, they are also impacted by city regulations and governance processes, but for the purposes here, we will focus on them as primarily actively engaged entities and a primary group in materializing smart city solutions.

Hardware vendors – It can be difficult to find pure hardware vendors as software is almost always a part of the product. The business of selling hardware is very different, since the company is rewarded for selling physical units primarily. Their interest is therefore tied to new deployment scenarios in the city. Often the offering comes wrapped with a full software solution, which means that they will try to make money of that too, but in general they will be motivated to sell as many units as possible regardless of whether they will exist in the long term. A special case of hardware vendors is telecommunications providers. Whereas they don't sell their hardware directly, the implementation and use of it is critically tied to cities allowing them to do it and using them for solution deployments.

Software vendors – Only sell their products embedded with hardware in exceptional cases like appliances or when they supply peripheral hardware like AWS and Microsoft offering an Internet of Things (IoT) button. Consequently, these vendors are interested in solutions where their software generates license, support, or subscription fees, which means they are interested in embedding their software in lasting solutions or as is the case with cloud vendors, to become the main platform for any type of solution. This means they are interested in integrating their solutions with other existing solutions to create durable long-term solutions or platforms.

Systems integrators – Are the ones who develop holistic discrete solutions that work from end to end. They are typically working on a project-based contract with a fixed number of deliverables. They are motivated to make the deployment as easy as possible and will often work toward a siloed solution, since it is easier when everything is isolated.

Government

Governments are groups of people authorized to develop and enforce policies in a sovereign area. Typically, it is split into a legislative, executive, and judiciary branch, but that need not be the case. It is also frequently divided into different layers with different authorities like the national, regional, and local governments.

- **National** – This level is not typically the most important for cities in the United States and Europe. National government may be interested in creating incentives for cities to develop smart city applications. This could be in the form of subsidizing certain types of development, or it could be in the form of grants to study and develop smart city solutions. In Asia, the situation is the reverse. In India and China, the smart city agenda is to a great extent driven from the top down by the national government.

- **Regional** – Many countries have a regional form of government with varying degrees of autonomy. The individual states in the United States or cantons in Switzerland are examples. Like the national government, they are rarely concerned with one particular city unless that city is central in their region, like New York City in the New York state. In this case, there can be a certain degree of interference between the interests at the regional and local levels.

- **Local** – Is the actual city level, which is the most important level for smart cities. The local level of government is directly affected by the successes and failures of smart city initiatives. This means that they are the most motivated to show progress. This, however, is also a case for concern since the mere fact of showing progress in the form of media stories and goodwill can sometimes limit the long-term effects of smart city initiatives.

Researchers

This group is interested in gaining knowledge in general and new insights in particular. Their primary interest is typically in experiments and data. They look for novelty and are rarely concerned with things such as deployment and scalability of solutions. There are a few variants:

- **Universities** – Are still the most prominent research institution since they have it as one of their main goals to do research. They sometimes struggle with the relevance of their research for the wider society. That said, there are different interests based on how universities are involved in smart cities:

  - Providing real-world problems as subject matter for students' projects

  - Internships for students

  - Research opportunities for scientific staff in the form of projects and collaborations

  - Paid research that generates revenue for the university

  - Grants that can help fund labs and staff

- **Private research** – These can be traditional think tanks and will typically have an interest in a particular niche subject. They are often more motivated by political incentives, for example, from special interest groups, than novelty, which is the main driver for universities. Private research typically ends up as reports that are published and promoted in the media.

- **Independent researchers** – These are sometimes similar to the citizen activists and are motivated by their own idiosyncratic ideas and concerns. This is where grassroots science is done.

Organizations

There are different types of organizations with an interest in smart cities, and they play major roles:

- **Supranational organizations** – Like the United Nations, World Bank, or the World Economic Forum, all have a great focus on cities since cities are important for their areas of interest. They do much the same thing as governments in that they develop policies and sponsor research, but they don't typically have any power to enforce policy directly. They are also to some degree similar to researchers since they sponsor research and study different aspects of smart cities.

- **Nongovernmental organizations** – These resemble the supranational organizations, but they don't necessarily have any support from any nations. They are typically devoted to one particular aspect like energy, clean tech, or sustainability. They can be an important resource for knowledge and also funding.

- **Philanthropies** – There are some philanthropic organizations whose primary purpose is to fund and sponsor rollout of smart city solutions. They typically have their own process and grants through which it is possible to get funding by submitting projects.

Areas of application of Smart City technology

Not all aspects of a city are equally relevant in a smart city context. Some areas are more susceptible to improvement with technology than others. Currently, the main focus of technological innovation and development can be divided into four areas: utilities, mobility, safety, and health and housing.

Utilities

This covers the basic functions of the city without which it would simply not be possible to sustain life at city scale. The utilities are the basic metabolic system of the city, but also it is an area with one of the largest environmental impacts. Consequently, much of current smart city initiatives have focused on this area.

- **Water** – Without sufficient clean water, humans cannot sustain life. This means that any gains in efficiency or quality are particularly valuable for the city. Since water is a scarce resource, minimizing waste is also often a focus area. McKinsey estimates that water consumption can be lowered by 20–30%. This can be done with smart meters and leakage control.

- **Energy** – Is a fundamental need for almost every function of the city, and cities are main consumers of energy on a global scale. Similar to water, energy is a scarce resource that we try to reduce with initiatives like dynamic electricity pricing and smart lighting solutions that turn light on and off depending on need.

- **Waste** – Removal of waste is central to making a city livable and healthy. Especially when cities have tourists, garbage removal is key. Cities want to minimize the resources used and look at solutions for optimizing routes for garbage trucks and automatic notifications when garbage bins are filled.

Mobility

Even though more opportunities for jobs, food, and entertainment are available in a city, they are rarely in close proximity to residential areas. This means that people depend on the city's offering of mobility services. Similarly, more people means more goods move into and out of the city. These are many and varied and currently the focus of a lot of innovation and new offerings. We see carpooling services, bike sharing, autonomous vehicles, scooters, and so on. Today there are multiple different ways for getting from point A to point B. Mobility seems to be one of the most blooming areas of city tech innovation, but there are still two primary areas that form the basis:

- **Public transit** – Regardless of the innovations we have considered, in many major cities, public transit is still a key form of mobility. Optimizing how mass transit flows and is utilized is therefore an important way to improve mobility. Since breakdowns in the transit system are often a prime cause of delays, predictive maintenance is another application that improves mobility.

- **Private transit** – The personal vehicle has still not died since it is unique in providing the greatest flexibility in terms of mobility. Congestion makes this a challenge for people and goods moving around. Consequently, smart city applications have targeted traffic regulation to avoid congestion. This can be through congestion pricing, taxing, or traffic regulation.

Safety

Keeping the businesses, residents, and visitors safe is a crucial goal for any city and an important parameter in the popularity and growth of a city.

- **Crime** – Increases disproportionally when cities grow larger and the people of the city will make no pause complaining about crime to the local government. The area of law enforcement is another area that has been early adopters of city technology with gunshot detection systems, body cams, and neighborhood policing solutions. But safety is more than combating crime.

- **Disasters** – Happen every day on a small scale. The fire department responds to fires, and ambulances take sick people to the hospital. Anything that can aid them in arriving earlier will help save lives. While these are smaller everyday or at least frequent occurrences, cities also need to prepare for larger shocks like volcanos, flooding, droughts, earthquakes, and hurricanes depending on their geographical location. But there are also manmade disasters like terrorism and general mismanagement. For these situations, technology can be crucial in mapping and understanding what is going on where.

Health

One of the most important areas for a city is health. This is one of the areas that already receives a lot of resources. Most of these are not dedicated to smart city solutions as such, but that does not mean that there will not be a need for it. One area of application is air quality monitoring and alerts, since the air quality is directly related to residents' health. The needs for technology to help in health-related contexts differ a lot depending on the climate the city is in but also on the type. An economically developed city like Vienna may have huge issues with cardiovascular diseases and not with infectious diseases, whereas the situation may be the reverse in Cape Town where a lot of residents do not have the same economic opportunities and access to basic medical aid. Understanding the different needs of cities to improve the health of their residents is helpful in determining the potential of technology to aid them.

Outline of the book

The book is divided into two parts. Part I is descriptive and aims to give the reader a basic understanding of technical aspects of smart cities. This resembles a classic textbook. Part II on the other hand is more prescriptive and aims to inspire smart city development and is closer to a collection of essays.

Chapter 2 is the first in Part I and treats the connectivity of the smart city. Here we will look at the different ways in which city technologies can be connected. First, we will consider the different types of networks that exist and look at their different properties and look at real-world examples of how connectivity is provided in cities.

Chapter 3 is about devices which are at the core of smart city solutions. We will consider what a device is and how they connect in distributed solutions. This is what is typically referred to as the Internet of Things. We look at the challenges of managing thousands or even millions of devices and what it takes to secure them.

Chapter 4 is about data. Some say data is the new oil; regardless of whether that is true, it is a crucial aspect to understand since all data is not the same and needs to be secured and managed differently. Recent increased concern about privacy and exponential growth in unstructured sensor data will be addressed.

Chapter 5 is about intelligence, in particular artificial intelligence (AI). AI offers a lot of potential in many aspects of human life also in the context of cities, but it is important to understand the different forces that affect adoption of AI solutions in a private and a public context.

Chapter 6 concerns engagement and will consider how we can engage the different actors in the smart city sphere. Different engagement models exist and have different advantages and challenges. We will look at how to choose the right one for a particular initiative.

Having understood the basics of smart city technology, it is time to consider what to do to start working toward smarter cities. Where we laid the basis in Part I for understanding the central elements of smart cities, in Part II we will look more into what we can do about it. Rather than offer a comprehensive and systematic agenda for what to do, the following are five recommendations that will get us started on the journey toward smarter cities. They explore key aspects and recommendations based on experience. The essays can also be read individually as sources of inspiration. They are meant to stimulate thought and action to promote smarter cities. We will focus primarily on enterprise architecture, data, and organizational issues. Other areas of focus could have been chosen, but I feel that these are key aspects.

In Chapter 7, the first recommendation is to "architect with imagination" because many opportunities are lost due to lack of imagination and a tendency to repeat what we have always been doing.

In order to escape this, we need to "make innovation a habit," which is the subject of Chapter 8. The reason for the current lack of imagination is just as much that we are lulled into the habits of what we are already doing.

Since cities run on data, we need to "build the data refinery." This is the focus of Chapter 9. Without extracting and cleaning the data, we will not be able to utilize it as a key resource for smart cities.

But clean data is not enough; we need to "optimize data value not just data quality." A framework for doing this is presented in Chapter 10.

In the end, we need an approach to make all this real. In Chapter 11, we look at how to implement real lasting change. This is not trivial; we need to "employ pragmatic idealism." This is a way that balances vision with practical results and provides some guidelines for action and how to select an appropriate team.

Summary

Cities are inextricably tied to human civilization. All the earliest civilizations grew forth from urban centers in the shape of city-states. The city has always been associated with technology in a reinforcing loop, where cities created the precondition for developing new technologies and were built using these new technologies. This is still the case today, only our technologies have become more advanced.

Historically, most of humankind have lived outside of cities, but within the last 50 years, we have reached an inflection point where more people live in cities than outside. The future promises a steady increase in urbanization on the global scale. We are at a point where we need to guide the use of technology to create the cities of tomorrow in the shape that we want them. The technology is there and will be used, but how we use it can either be in an ad hoc way or in a guided and goal-oriented fashion. Most smart city development has so far been unstructured and ad hoc.

It can be difficult to get an overview of smart cities literature and implementations. While there are many definitions, here we focus on understanding how technology can help a city deal with challenges and provide opportunities for its residents so as to make it a more sustainable, resilient, and livable city.

In order to do this, we need to understand the main components of smart cities: the actors and primary areas of application. The different groups of actors – individuals, businesses, vendors, government, researchers, and organizations – all have their particular focus and strengths. It is important to know that in order to engage them optimally. Currently, the four main areas where we see smart city technologies being applied are utilities, mobility, safety, and health. These are very different areas with different opportunities and challenges.

PART I

Understanding smart cities

CHAPTER 2

Connectivity

For smart city technologies to have any impact, they need to be connected. Here we will look at the different ways in which city technologies can be connected. We will look at different types of network, their properties and dynamics, as well as typical applications in a smart city context. We will also look at the different ways devices can be connected to each other and different networks like the Internet.

Few devices, gadgets, or computers are interesting in isolation. Devices in a smart city context are usually made for a specific purpose and form part of a larger system of distributed computing. In distributed computing, the computation of the system is done not only in the central processing unit of one computer but in multiple discrete units. When they are connected, they form a network. Different networks have different properties that impact the performance and resilience of the entire distributed system. A well-known term for this type of computing is the Internet of Things or IoT for short. However, it is important to step back and remember that smart city technology does not need to be based on the Internet. The Internet is just one type of connection and network, but there are other types. It is important at this point not to confuse the abstract use of the word network that we will consider in this section with the technical and specific one of computer networks. These are special implementations of networks.

The science of networks is called *graph theory* which has been around since the Eighteenth century as a mathematical discipline with Leonhard Euler writing the first paper on the subject in the start of the century.

© Anders Lisdorf 2020
A. Lisdorf, *Demystifying Smart Cities*, https://doi.org/10.1007/978-1-4842-5377-9_2

While this did yield interesting insights and hypotheses especially in the Twentieth century, it wasn't until the turn of the millennium through the work of Duncan Watts when the mathematics were rigorously reconciled with empirical observations, thereby improving the science of connectivity. Now we know that the type of network impacts the real-world properties and dynamics in nontrivial ways.

Network topologies

A network is made up of nodes and links that connect them. A node is a single entity in a network. For reference, in a social network, a node is an individual. The link is something that connects them, which would be an accepted friend request in an online social network. This would be seen as a list of friends, which is a list of links to other nodes. The characteristics of how network nodes connect to other nodes are called *network topologies*. There are a few different basic types of topologies that are used in different situations.

Point-to-point topology

This is the simplest possible topology since it just consists of two nodes connected by a single link. For those who can remember the standard landline telephone or two cans connected by a string that kids used to make, these are examples of point-to-point networks. When you dial another phone number, you connect to it directly. No other telephones are included. See Figure 2-1 for a depiction of this topology.

Figure 2-1. Point-to-point topology

Although it seems quite vacuous in our age where webs of connections are a valuable thing, it is much more widespread than you might think. One of the reasons for this is that it can be incredibly secure. If you connect to one and only one other node, no one else will be able to get to the information. This is the principle behind VPN (Virtual Private Network) tunnels. When you connect to another machine through a VPN tunnel, it guarantees that the information exchanged is exchanged only between these two nodes. Another widespread point-to-point technology is FTP (file transfer protocol). Here you need to add encryption to make sure that no one is eavesdropping though.

One of the most well-known and ubiquitous technologies that utilizes this topology is Bluetooth. See Table 2-1 for a list of topology features. As anyone who has tried to battle their children for access to the wireless system in the car to listen to music will know, it only accepts a connection to one phone. This type of connection is well suited for connections at short distances, which is also utilized in the NFC (Near Field Communication) technologies of chips on payment cards, smart watches, and phones.

Table 2-1. *Point-to-point topology highlights*

Point-to-Point	
Key properties	Simple, secure, not scalable
Good for	Connection at short distances, exclusive connectivity
Technologies	Bluetooth, NFC, VPN
Examples	Payment with a smart watch, phone, or chip in card. Connecting a cell phone to a device to control it

Tree topology

In a tree topology, the nodes link in a hierarchical fashion. Each node has a number of child nodes. This means that nodes at the bottom do not have the same connective properties as those at the top. To put it in a different way: nodes toward the top of the tree have a bigger exposure to other nodes than nodes toward the bottom (Figure 2-2).

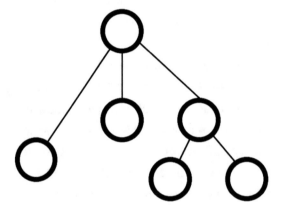

Figure 2-2. *Tree topology*

It can be very fast and efficient to propagate information to the right node if the route can be based on heuristics embedded in the tree structure. This means that if the tree is structured according to a routing logic, it can be very fast and simple to route information to the right target. For example, if the first layer consists of nodes named after numbers, the next layer is with the letters of the alphabet, and the third layer divides up nodes according to Roman numerals. This is the structure of bullet point lists (see the following):

1. First node of the first layer

    a. First node of the second layer

        i.   First node of the third layer

        ii. Second node of the third layer

        iii. Third node of the third layer

    b. Second node of the second layer

    c. Third node of the second layer

2. Second node of the first layer

3. Third node of the first layer

Now, if you want to route information to [1aiii], it is very fast since the information just needs to follow the route of the tree. In a bus topology, it would have to follow the bus and check the address of every node to see if it matches. In a star topology, all traffic has to go through the center, which taxes the central node bandwidth – more on bus and star topology later in the chapter.

This means that information travelling top-down or bottom-up is efficient, but for information travelling across, it has to traverse the tree up first and then down and is a lot more difficult.

Another thing to keep in mind is that trees are susceptible to single point of failure vulnerabilities. If the top node fails, the whole network fails. Similarly for each branch of the tree, if a root node for a branch fails, all of the nodes on the branch and subbranches will fail. See Table 2-2 for more tree topology features.

Table 2-2. *Tree topology highlights*

Tree	
Key properties	Fast propagation of information but necessary to know the tree structure to get information across, Single point of failure
Good for	Problems that have a hierarchical structure or information structures where changes to the network structure at the root and top levels are rare but frequent at lower levels
Technologies	DNS, Greengrass, IoT Edge
Examples	Decision trees, device gateways, Internet DNS structure

One system that is built according to a tree topology is none other than the Internet or more accurately the Domain Name System (DNS) according to which URLs get resolved to actual machine IP addresses. The DNS is anchored in the top node called the *root name server*. Due to the vulnerability of the tree topology, this was distributed to 13 different physical root name servers. This server keeps the names of the next level, the "top-level domains or TLDs." These are the well-known .com, .org, and .edu as well as the country-specific domains like .fr, .it, and .dk. Each of these top-level domains has a domain server as well. On this server, the registrar who manages the Internet domain creates the web addresses we know and remember like wikipedia.org and points them to a specific IP address of the owner's choice. The owner of the domain name then in turn has its own server and manages subdomains.

Tree structures can be seen when multiple devices connect to a common gateway that then connects to the Internet. This is the principle for AWS's Greengrass or Azure's IoT Edge. Here, a number of devices connect to a Greengrass device, which then connects to the Internet. This is either because they don't have enough power or bandwidth themselves to connect to the Internet or because it is more cost-effective. Similar solutions are set up with software in local wifi routers, and solutions using Software-Defined Networks also frequently employ a hierarchical structure.

Bus topology

The bus topology gets its name from the Latin *omnibus* which means "for all." In a bus topology, the nodes all connect to a central bus through which all information flows (see Figure 2-3). Each node sends information along the line of the bus. Each node checks if the information is addressed to it. If it is not, it is ignored and the information passes on to the next node on the line.

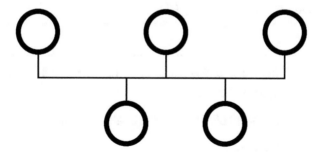

Figure 2-3. *Bus topology*

This may be familiar from the Local Area Network (LAN) that most people have in their homes or at their job. When you plug the cord into the LAN, it is connected to all the other nodes that are connected. This means that you can now send files to be printed or use the shared network folders.

This architecture is also used centrally in computers on the motherboard with the PCI protocol. Here, the different components of a computer like memory, CPU, graphic card, and sound card are connected through a bus. This bus is implemented physically on the print card.

One key property of the bus topology is that it is easy to connect a node to the network. See Table 2-3 for more bus topology highlights. The node just needs to connect to the bus and be able to navigate the address space. On the other hand, the bus topology is vulnerable because the bus is a single point of failure. If the connection along a bus breaks, it does not mean that the whole network fails like the star topology, but it means that the network is partitioned into two segments. If information needs to travel from a node in one segment to a node in the other, it is not possible, but within a segment, it is still possible. This type of problem is sometimes overcome in a variant of the bus topology called a ring topology where the bus connects like a ring and information travels in both directions. In this case, the information will get to the node the other way around the ring.

Table 2-3. *Bus topology highlights*

Bus	
Key properties	Simple to add new nodes to the network, Failure causes network segmentation
Good for	Most distributed problems that are not vulnerable to failure
Protocols	DSL, Ethernet
Examples	Traffic cameras, broadband, motherboard

This type of network structure is versatile, which is why it is widespread in distributed computing, but it is best suited for problems that are not vulnerable to network segmentation and unavailability.

In a smart city context, we see this used for traffic monitoring solutions. The cameras will often be connected to a closed circuit of a traffic monitoring and control unit. It is easy to go out and plug another camera in. Broadband is also based on a bus topology where the cable is typically coaxial or fiber optic.

Star topology

The star topology is also called a hub and spoke structure due to its similarity to a wheel. A simple example of a solution that works according to this would be a shared Google doc. The document is the center, the hub, through which all information is passed between the users. I once had a class of more than 60 students writing on the same Google doc as an assignment. The information one person wrote was transferred through the Google doc serving as the hub to all the others. This was a star topology in action. Another example even more ubiquitous is the wifi router. All the home wireless devices like phones, tablets, computers, and printers connect to this central hub, which in turn acts as a gateway to the Internet. See an illustration of the star topology in Figure 2-4.

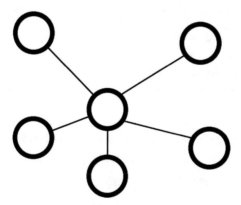

Figure 2-4. *Star topology*

The star topology is similar to the tree in that it has a root node and multiple connected nodes. It differs in that it never has branches. Technically, a tree is a recursive star topology. It has also been very popular in the history of computing. The original mainframes operated in this way where workstations connected to the mainframe and interacted with it. This is also the model known as the client-server model, which dominated computing for decades. It forms the backbone of the HTTP protocol. A web server handles HTTP requests like GET or PUT. Any browser who knows the IP address (which the DNS structure mentioned in the preceding text helps resolve) of the web server may connect to it in a client-server type of network. In this manner, information can be posted to a web page on the server, retrieved, deleted, or updated for all other clients to see.

As the use for the HTTP protocol shows, the star topology is very good for brokering information and making it easily accessible to many different consumers, since each node in the network need only link to one other node: the hub. This means that nodes in general need to have minimal knowledge of the network topology.

Another property to be aware of is that it is a single point of failure. If the central node becomes unavailable, all nodes are unavailable. If you have ever heard the phrase "the server is down" spread like a wildfire through the room, this is the sound of a single point of failure. Table 2-4 details the star topology features.

Table 2-4. *Star topology highlights*

Star	
Key properties	Easy to connect a node to the entire network, single point of failure, all traffic has to go through the center node, Minimal knowledge of network structure necessary
Good for	Information brokering, information exchange
Technologies	HTTP, MQTT, Pub/Sub, Kafka,
Examples	Device gateways, fleet management, streaming solutions

There are a few applications of this structure in a smart city context as well. Since the number of devices is increasing, it becomes technically and economically unfeasible to equip each sensor with a SIM card. Instead information is aggregated through connections to a so-called device gateway. This increases the performance of the network since the devices can be focused on simple local transactions with the gateway and the gateway can aggregate and route data through the Internet.

Another example is fleet information systems. The individual vehicles in a fleet are equipped with a sensor that connects with a server that records the data about the vehicle's location as well as additional telemetry data about the operation of the vehicle.

For many IoT implementations, sending data in a streaming format is key. This is often done with Publish-Subscribe types of architectures. Here the source system publishes to a topic that clients can subscribe to. The broker who facilitates this acts as a hub that "hosts" the different topics to which connected nodes can publish and subscribe.

A well-known technology to support this is the open source project Kafka. This is often used for streaming data and works around a central broker to which clients connect. Information is published to the broker on a topic which other clients can follow. This is used for many big data solutions.

A standard protocol in IoT implementations is the MQTT protocol. This works in a similar fashion with a broker and devices publishing their information to the broker on a topic. In turn they follow other topics to listen for instructions. It was specifically developed to be lightweight and allow devices to communicate telemetry data.

Mesh topology

In a mesh network, nodes connect directly and nonhierarchically to each other. In a fully connected mesh network, all nodes are connected to all nodes, but typically mesh networks are not fully connected. This is the kind of network we know as social networks, where people connect to each other and the network as such can have varying degrees of connectivity (see Figure 2-5).

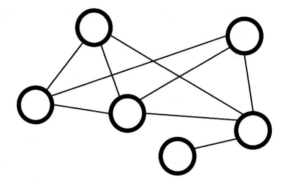

Figure 2-5. *Mesh topology*

Those of us who are old enough to remember the service called Napster will recognize that this was indeed a competing network structure to the World Wide Web. Napster was a peer-to-peer service where each computer was open directly for contact with other computers. The purpose of Napster was to share music, so if you searched for a specific song, you could look through the network of connected computers that were on at the time to locate the song you were looking for. You could then connect directly to that computer and download the song. Similarly, other computers could connect to your computer and download your songs.

The mesh network is a very resilient type of network because it usually is not susceptible to a single point of failure or partitions in the network. If one node, even a central node, is down, information can usually find its way through the other nodes. The challenge for a node in a mesh network is to locate the target node.

Anyone familiar with the 6 degrees of separation problem will know that the theory is that everyone on earth is connected by on average 6 degrees to each other. This means that any random person will be able to reach any other random person on average through six intermediary connections. All nodes are similarly closely linked. Compare this to the bus topology where information has to pass through the bus node by node until it reaches the one it is searching for. In a mesh network, each node has to know a number of other nodes.

The mesh network is good for problems where resilience is a key factor. It is the optimal network topology for solutions that need to be highly available even in times of shock. It is also great at information distribution where the target node is not known in advance since it can go through a minimum number of hops to get there. See Table 2-5 for a list of mesh network features.

Table 2-5. *Mesh topology highlights*

Mesh	
Key properties	Resilient, interconnected, information can get around through few hops, self-organized
Good for	Resilient networks that scale well. Geographically challenging distributed connected solutions
Technologies	B.A.T.M.A.N., Zigbee
Examples	Irrigation solutions, building management systems

Since not all nodes in a mesh network need to reach a central controller, they are particularly good for geographically distributed problems. One example is irrigation of public parks. Rather than have each moisture sensor connect to the Internet, only a few nodes in the network need to act as Internet gateways. This way information is routed through the network until it reaches a gateway node.

It can also be used inside buildings for wireless electric meters and HVAC or underground where cellular connections are difficult. By making sure devices are connected in a mesh, this type of network can penetrate areas that other types of connection cannot.

The B.A.T.M.A.N., or Better Approach To Mobile Adhoc Networking, is an example of a popular protocol for routing data on a mesh network and so is Zigbee, which is frequently used for indoor connected devices.

Connecting devices

Now that we have considered different types of networks, let us look at how the links between nodes are typically established from a technical perspective at the physical layer. There are two basic ways of connecting devices: wired and wireless. Each comes in a different variant, but they are still fairly similar.

Cables come in a few different forms: copper and fiber optic cables are the most common. We see these going into our router and maybe between computers. On the other hand, we do not see wireless connections, but they are equally well known in the form of wifi, 4G, and Bluetooth. These are all actually just different types of radio. Indeed virtually all forms of wireless communication are based on radio technology with signals of varying range and frequency. One exception is optical connections where information is communicated through a laser beam.

Once there is a physical connection between two nodes, the network can be built out to include more nodes. The key thing to be aware of is how the nodes connect.

The anatomy of a connection

Regardless of how a connection is implemented, there are some regularities in how we can conceptualize it. These are captured by the seven-layer OSI model. This model is the product of an ISO (International Organization for Standardization) project and is widely referred to in computer networking. The purpose of the model is to abstract the physical implementation and use common protocols so different implementations of networking would be interoperable. This is why the Internet works just as well over cable as wifi or cellular from the point of view of the end user.

The layers are constructed such that they encapsulate a particular function and only communicate with the layer above and below. The outer layer that faces the user is layer 7, and the lower physical layer where the bits hit the wire is layer 1. The details are rarely relevant, since most IoT applications today interface at layer 7. However, it is not bound to remain that way, since the lower you get, the less the computational overhead. Already today many smart city applications connect on layer 4. See Table 2-6.

Table 2-6. *The OSI model*

Layer	Name	Function	Protocols
7	Application	The interface for applications, where we find the API	HTTP, FTP, MQTT
6	Presentation	Encoding into binary format and encrypts. Provides independence by translating from the application format to the network format	MIME, SSL, TLS
5	Session	Handles connections between devices	NetBIOS
4	Transport	Divides data into packets for transport on the network	TCP, UDP
3	Network	Provides ability to transport data on the network	IPv4, IPv6, IPSec, Zigbee, LoRaWAN
2	Data Link	The transmission between two nodes on the network	Ethernet, IEEE 802.11
1	Physical	Encodes digital format to physical transmission medium	LoRa, Bluetooth, USB

When two devices communicate with each other, the process starts at the top layer: the application layer. One of the devices initiates a communication at the application layer with a top-level protocol like HTTP that we use for Internet communication. This is then passed down the layers until it is a physical stream of binary data at the lowest level. Here it travels to the other devices which receive it at the lowest level and piece the information together up the layers until the initial data is received.

The top layer, layer 7, is the one that is closest to the user. Applications have their different logic and functions, but in this layer, data gets wrapped in one of the available standard protocols by the application.

The next layer is the presentation layer, which may be a bit misleading in its name since it does not present anything. It translates the application layer's data to another format, which is why it is also sometimes called the syntax layer.

The fifth layer is the session layer and handles everything related to creating, maintaining, and terminating connections between computers and devices. A session is useful since data has to be converted to a stream and transmitted. The session makes sure that the connection is established and open for the whole data load.

The fourth layer is the transport layer and handles how data is sent. Some protocols like TCP handle situations where data is lost in transmission and resends them, while others like UDP just sends the data and disregards whether the user receives it or not.

The third layer, the network layer, encapsulates the means for transferring data packets. The individual packets are usually too small to contain an entire message and need to be pieced together. At the network layer, the only thing that is necessary to specify is data and a destination address. The most well-known protocol here is the Internet Protocol.

Layer 2 is the link layer where a link between two nodes is established. This is where most of the protocols for communication work. Some well-known ones are Ethernet, wifi, and Zigbee. These all have different properties in terms of range and bandwidth.

The lowest level is responsible for transmission of raw data between a device and a physical medium like a cable or radio transmitter. It converts the data into electrical, radio, or optical signals. There are different types of cables like the twisted pair known from standard phone wires, coaxial cables used for TV connections, and the fiber optic ones. Similarly, there are different types of wireless connections like radio waves, microwaves, and infrared that all have different properties, which make them useful in different contexts. See Table 2-7 for more information on the properties of different types of physical connections.

Table 2-7. *Properties of different types of physical connection*

Connection Type	Advantages	Disadvantages	Used for
Wired connections			
Twisted pair	Inexpensive	Low bandwidth, short distance transmission	Telephony, Ethernet
Coaxial	Inexpensive, high bandwidth, noise immune	Expensive to install	Broadband, cable TV
Fiber optic	Vastly greater bandwidth, long distance, long life span	Fragile, expensive	Broadband, Internet
Wireless connections			
Radio waves	Penetrates buildings, antennas need not be aligned	Spectrum is a limited resource and regulated	AM and FM radios, cordless phones, cellular network, wifi router
Microwaves	Long range	Antennas need to be aligned	Mobile phone communication, television
Infrared	Only very short distances	Cannot penetrate obstacles	Remotes, wireless keyboard and mouse

Solution spotlights

LinkNYC

In 2012, New York City decided that the city's more than 10,000 payphones should be replaced. The franchising agreement for the public payphones was due to expire by the end of 2014. The New York Department of IT and Telecommunications sent out a Request for Information in which they asked for suggestions as to how existing payphones could be converted and alternative uses of the sidewalk capacity be made such as "Wi-Fi antennas that would create public wireless hotspots, touch-screen wayfinding panels, information kiosks, charging stations for mobile communications devices, electronic community bulletin boards, or other types of innovative sidewalk amenities."

This resulted in the LinkNYC kiosks that are now ubiquitous in New York. These are the product of a partnership called CityBridge, consisting of Intersection, who produces the kiosks, Qualcomm, and CIVIQ Smartscapes. The implementation is funded 100% by advertising on the kiosks, which means that no taxpayer money is going toward supporting it.

The LinkNYC kiosks offer connection to wifi for the public's various devices. The wifi is fast and free. The wifi routers in the kiosks are connected to the Internet through optical fiber cables so as to make sure the bandwidth is sufficient. Internet connection to the city's services can also be accessed through the tablets. This means that the LinkNYC kiosks are essentially decentralized hubs that connect to the Internet. But it is also connected to the phone system and allows users to place phone calls and has a 911 button for emergencies.

Even the advertising displays have been coopted for city service in that they display information relevant for the city at some frequency and in times of emergency, like the steam pipe explosion in July 2018, are able to display evacuation routes to the public and other pertinent information.

The LinkNYC concept was completely new when it was deployed in New York, but has been adopted by several other cities like London and Philadelphia. It shows how a traditional mode of connection, the phone, can be reconceptualized to a new and more contemporary way of connecting through wifi. What is also interesting is how the city engaged with an industry partnership to produce the service at zero cost to taxpayers even creating more than 100 jobs along the way. This is an example of a multiple win-win situation that not only is cost neutral to develop and maintain but creates increased prosperity and resilience for the city while making connectivity free and accessible for all.

The Things Network: LoRaWAN

The Things Network is an open source decentralized network to support the Internet of Things. It is using the LoRaWAN protocol to connect devices across the world. LoRaWAN is short for Long Range Wide Area Network and one of the most widely adopted Low Power Wide Area Networks. It is a network player protocol that builds on the physical layer LoRa protocol. Version 1 was released in 2015. It works at a 10+ kilometer range, and since it is low power, devices can last for years without changing batteries. The downside is that the data rate is very limited at around a few hundred bps. Compare this to wifi which is up to 200 mbps, that is, almost a million times more throughput. It is therefore not suitable for Netflix or phone calls but okay for devices with a low amount of information exchange that does not need to be real time like a sensor. The Things Network uses MQTT as the layer 7 protocol by which devices communicate.

It uses unlicensed parts of the lower end of the radio spectrum, which is why it can be used for free. The radio spectrum is cut up in ever smaller chunks, and companies pay billions of dollars for it, which is a prohibitive factor for many applications to scale the solution. An LTE connection is basically a cell phone connection and therefore carries the same price. If you want to implement thousands of sensors, it may be too costly.

Devices in The Things Network can connect to each other or to a gateway. The gateway is connected to the Internet through wifi or Ethernet or some other medium. When a device broadcasts a signal, it is received by all gateways within reach, and later the signal is deduplicated. This is a mesh topology that provides increased resilience because if one gateway misses the signal, another one can pick it up. If you want to increase resilience in an area, you just add additional gateways.

The initiative is a good example of a bottom-up approach that is not guided by any government or industry leaders. Still, it has been used for utility meters, solar-powered smart bus schedules, and smart parking sensors.

NYC Mesh

Internet connectivity is becoming a basic necessity in cities, but too often the incumbent service providers overcharge and underdeliver. In New York City under Mayor Bill de Blasio, the administration is already pursuing a goal of providing affordable high-speed broadband by 2025 to remedy this situation. However, this is also approached from the bottom up through initiatives like NYC Mesh and Silicon Harlem that aim to offer free or low-cost high-speed Internet. Furthermore, NYC Mesh aims to fill pockets in the city that the service providers have not yet covered with Internet.

The way they do this is through a mesh network of routers that connect to a hub node or a supernode. The supernode is connected to the Internet and has a number of other antennas. The hub node is not connected directly to the Internet but does so through supernodes. Routers can connect to the hub node in a neighborhood. This way there are multiple paths to the Internet. In the event that the Internet is down, the mesh network would still connect the individual nodes locally. NYC Mesh sells routers, hubs, and supernodes and charges a small fee for installation on rooftops and asks users to donate $20 per month for their connection.

The technology used for connectivity between nodes is a directional antenna to enhance the range of the connection, but it also means that the nodes need to have line of sight of each other. Routers can be connected to computers through Ethernet cables like regular computers.

The NYC Mesh initiative shows how grassroots civic activists are able to deliver on the same promises that the city's elected officials make. The network also has another property that is particularly interesting for New Yorkers, that is, resiliency. After 9/11 all communication was down for days leaving residents and city employees trying to coordinate help with no Internet or phone. Subsequently hundreds of millions have been spent on the city's own proprietary wifi network: NYCWiN. This is now being decommissioned due to high operating costs. NYC Mesh, if built out, would provide the resilience that New York was looking for in the NYCWiN network, and with the budget NYCWiN used, this could be done easily. This case also shows how even when stakeholders are aligned on the goals and a solution has been demonstrated to work, it may still not be straightforward to cooperate and develop it.

Summary

Networks exist at multiple different levels in nature in general and in smart city solutions in particular. It is important to understand the network topology regardless of the level it is implemented in because it has significant implications for the properties and dynamics of the solution as a whole. The primary types of network topologies are point-to-point, tree, bus, star, and mesh. Some networks are prone to a single point of failure but very fast and efficient, whereas others may be slower but more resilient. Some are more well suited for certain types of problems than others. Choosing the right network topology for the solution is important for the success of any connected smart city solution.

There are also multiple choices to make the physical connection between devices. A key framework to understand is the OSI model with its seven layers as this is a framework that permeates all connectivity solutions in smart city deployments. There are different protocols and functions at each level.

It is also important to decide whether a connection should be wired or wireless. Both have advantages and in practice both will be used for most implementations. It is however worthwhile to consider the properties of the different types of connection as this impacts everything from latency over resilience to cost.

CHAPTER 3

Devices

To many people, a device is a phone, smart watch, or tablet, but in a city context, the examples of devices exceed these. Devices are at the core of smart city solutions and therefore important to get a handle on. In this chapter, we will consider what a device is and how devices connect in distributed smart city solutions. This is what is typically referred to as the Internet of Things. We look at the challenges of managing thousands or even millions of devices and what it takes to secure them. We will also consider examples of how to build standards around the use of devices in a city context.

Even the casual observer of the world of technology has heard about the Internet of Things or IoT for short. To many people, IoT is this magical thing that will manage our homes, mow our lawns, and bring us the food we need when we need it. This may indeed be one of the end results, but before we get there, we should consider what this really means. In the previous chapter, we broke down different ways to connect things. But what exactly is connected? What are these "things" that are connected in the Internet of Things? A more precise term than "thing" might be device, since most of the things we are thinking about in the context of IoT are devices.

Using IoT solutions has become commonplace for cities. Examples of these are smart trash cans that can signal when they are full, smart water meters that can report water consumption in real time, and intelligent light poles that turn on only when people are present. These solutions allow us to minimize the amount of human labor in a number of tedious tasks,

© Anders Lisdorf 2020
A. Lisdorf, *Demystifying Smart Cities*, https://doi.org/10.1007/978-1-4842-5377-9_3

but also allow us to do things at a greater scale with greater intelligence. Consider traffic counts: most cities need to manually count traffic to understand the flow of traffic in central corridors. This is a tedious and resource-intensive task, since you need a human to manually count each vehicle. IoT offers alternatives such as counting vehicles by pneumatic tubes on the ground, infrared light, and radar or using computer vision built in to cameras. This can be done at a much bigger scale, since humans need to go and sleep every once in a while, whereas devices never sleep and will keep counting when they are set up, and they will be doing it at a lower cost. This makes devices an attractive alternative for cities.

However, devices are also liabilities in terms of security. There are rarely any enforced basic standards on devices, and security is frequently up to the discretion of the manufacturer. Implementations are also frequently ad hoc and siloed making it harder to harvest the full potential of IoT solutions for the city. Consequently, devices are a central focus area in the smart city landscape today. We therefore need to understand the level of the device in order to be able to use them more productively to create smarter cities.

What is a device?

A device is often thought of in consumer terms as a gadget with multiple functions like a cell phone, e-reader, or smart watch, but it can be much simpler. It does not need to be much more than a sensor attached to some sort of equipment. We typically divide devices into two classes: sensors and actuators. The sensors register some aspect of their environment like temperature, moisture, movement, or light. An actuator on the other hand does something to its environment like increase temperature and light or perform an action like closing a door. In short, with connected devices, we can combine sensors and actuators to create distributed computational systems that interact with and regulate our environment without human

46

intervention. Most frequently, there is also a need to process or relay the readings that the device makes from the environment or the actions it needs to perform. See Figure 3-1 for an illustration.

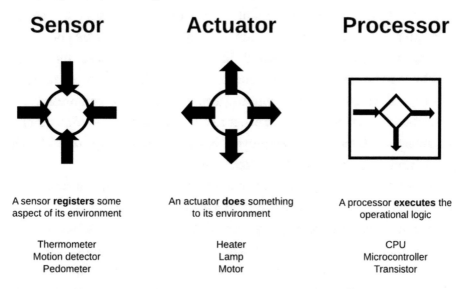

Sensor	Actuator	Processor
A sensor **registers** some aspect of its environment	An actuator **does** something to its environment	A processor **executes** the operational logic
Thermometer	Heater	CPU
Motion detector	Lamp	Microcontroller
Pedometer	Motor	Transistor

Figure 3-1. *Sensor and actuator*

Today, a popular way of building distributed systems of sensors and actuators is through a computer. This is what we also know from the laptop, tablet, and cell phones. This is essentially an integrated system with multiple components like memory, a CPU, and different ports to which sensors can be connected. Numerous devices work with a computer since it is convenient. Our fitness apps are based on a smartphone, the self-service kiosk based on a tablet, and so on. These are all solutions that are built around sensors, actuators, and processors. There are also popular inexpensive platforms for this like the Raspberry Pi. It does not have the screen, but it can be connected to one. It runs the ubiquitous Linux operating system and is programmable with Python and other standard programming languages. This means that most programmers will be able to integrate devices and make experiments and IoT solutions. It is also easy to connect to the Internet with standard wifi or cellular network.

This is the pattern of hobbyists and also a number of startup companies, but frequently the size of a device does not afford the luxury of a large and clunky Raspberry Pi computer even if it is small for a computer. Consider the first wave of successful medical devices, for example: hearing aids and pacemakers. These are almost microscopic devices that do not fit a computer. They use embedded chips such as microprocessors. Since they need to be small and very robust in function, they are not amenable to the usual type of programming, and a special kind of programming for embedded systems exists. In order to make these devices work, other languages like C are usually employed. Working with this type of devices is much more challenging and time-consuming.

Another interesting contrast to computers is that microcontrollers are special purpose, whereas computers are general purpose. A microcontroller needs to be programmed for a specific task. While they can be updated, it is a challenging operation since they are embedded in the device. An air quality sensor, for example, is meant to only ever measure air quality and may have a microcontroller built in to gather and relay data through the Internet. It is purpose built and optimized for this particular goal. A computer on the other hand is made for everything from watching Netflix over playing chess games to writing poetry in a word processor or finding the best vacations online. A device is an analog to a bacteria or fungus made for one specific kind of environment using only very specific inputs and outputs where computers are like mammals that adapt to a number of different environments.

At the lowest level, an integrated circuit can be thought of as a processor too. We know them from old-fashioned electronics like a stereo. They still serve a purpose where the processing logic is not likely to change, since the logic is physically implemented in the circuit board and not programmed through a programming language. For an overview of the characteristics of the different types of processing unit see Table 3-1.

Table 3-1. *Different types of processing units*

	Compute Flexibility	Development	Processing Logic	Energy Consumption
Computer	Very flexible	Easy	Complex	High
Microcontroller	Rigid	Medium	Complex	Medium
Integrated circuits	Fixed	Hard	Simple	Low

Working with devices in the city

Cities typically employ a number of devices in specialized solutions like traffic monitoring, air quality and water contamination measurements, and so on, but it is rare that any centralized governance or architecture has ever been put in place around how to build distributed systems with devices or how to manage them. The reason for this is that IoT solutions are typically bought by lines of business with a particular problem in mind, like showing the progress of snow plows in the winter. This becomes a political priority, and something has to be done fast and efficiently. Consequently, the project is conceptualized and procured outside the usual technology procurement and implementation processes that are in place.

The effect of this is that many smart city implementations today are ragtag collections of devices that have little if any interoperability and are difficult to manage. They have been procured by somebody with a tactical need in a particular domain, but not according to any overall central technology initiative or strategic vision. This is important to keep in mind when working with smart city technology, because it poses a number of architectural challenges that can prove very costly to work with. These isolated and siloed implementations that were originally innovative and forward looking become blockers for further smart city implementations.

To reach back to the introduction of this book: this is an example of how the smart city landscape today is built according to "the Way of the Pack Donkey" following the path of least resistance and little or no central planning and coordination.

Another reason for this lack of central governance and control of IoT implementations is a skill gap in central technology organizations. A central technology organization in a city is typically an IT department. They were built at a time when computing and digitalization of business processes were expanding and are focused on core traditional technology initiatives like running a data center, providing computers to employees, and developing and maintaining information systems like financial and HR systems. Very little of this work can be generalized or reused when faced with a device that has its very own unique and peculiar way of functioning. No wonder that implementations are primarily made by specialized contractors.

Managing devices

While it is wonderful what we can do with devices, they are also a major challenge in many cases. With computer systems, we are used to a structured change management process where upgrades or changes to functionality are periodically carried out. Typically, IT systems in a city context have a service window, systems to deploy new versions of the code exist, and it is easy to roll back if something goes wrong. Take for example an accounting system. No one is using this system Sunday night, so it can be completely closed down and upgraded. When it boots, employees test it, and if it doesn't work, the city can just go back to the old version and correct the update.

For devices all of this is a luxury that cannot be afforded. Consider the pacemaker again; who would sign up for a pacemaker with a service window of a few hours on Sunday nights? Even for less critical ones like water meters, it is difficult to find a mechanism to deploy new code. Remember that embedded systems usually come precoded from the factory and are typically not made to be updated ever again.

One thing is updates but another is the basic connectivity. Usually you want to have some sort of connection to a device and either get readings if it is a sensor or control it if it is an actuator. One of the first natural concerns should be security. When a device was on a closed network, this was not an issue, since the perimeter-based security of the network made sure that no one could gain access to the device. We will return to this aspect in a later section. Consider security cameras. They were originally closed circuit or at least on a cabled internal network connected to a control room where you could watch feeds from the cameras. In recent times, security cameras became IP cameras that were based on the Internet, which is great because you don't have to worry so much about building out the network and adding new cameras. They are all on the Internet and easy to reach from any computer with Internet connection. However, this means that the security that the perimeter of the network gave is now gone. Now connectivity to the device cannot be assumed to be trusted. In order to keep protecting the confidentiality of the device, there needs to be a mechanism for this beyond just knowledge of the endpoint address. Authentication becomes important for devices when they are on the Internet and no longer behind a firewall on an internal network.

There are good and well-proven solutions for this, like using certificates to authenticate and establish a trusted connection. All the major cloud platforms have some sort of platform to manage devices. AWS has the AWS IoT platform, Azure the IoT Hub. These are great and very safe and easy to work with and allow you to do pretty much anything you would want to do with a device. They all employ some way to initialize a connection to a device and receive streams of data from it. You can find excellent tutorials on how to connect devices like the AWS IoT button, which are fun and enlightening. You will see compelling demos at the vendors' events. But when you want to manage devices in a smart city context, scalability quickly becomes an issue that they do not demo on stage or in tutorials. When you move beyond proof of concept (POC) and pilot implementations with a handful of devices, the game changes radically.

A city like New York has more than 30,000 vehicles in its fleet. Each vehicle has a device to track its location. It also has hundreds of thousands of water meters. From personal experience, it takes even a good programmer 10–20 minutes to connect one device to an IoT platform. Just configuring the connection to the fleet would in the best case take 5000 hours using the approach by major cloud platforms today. That would mean two developers for more than a year. Although New York is bigger than most cities, clearly some different mechanism has to be employed in order to scale smart city implementations involving devices.

The big tech vendors who sell IoT platforms do not at the time of writing have any great solutions out of the box for doing this at scale, which is an important limitation when considering using their platforms as the basis for smart city initiatives. This is part of the reason that IoT solutions are often procured end to end from specialized vendors.

The market for IoT platforms, however, is not just made out of the established tech vendors, but an incredible array of smaller specialized so-called IoT platforms exist. This is a jungle, and it is probably a good idea to wait for the market to stabilize before making any far-reaching decisions about IoT platform strategy. Even large vendors suddenly drop out of the market or reorient their offering. Having one central IoT platform for all things IoT is a challenge since the market for IoT platforms is still very immature. This does not mean that the solutions are immature or not technically sound. Quite the contrary, many good solutions exist; they are just not tied together very well. It is therefore to be expected that cities will have multiple IoT platforms in the near future in order to support their needs.

Methods for communicating with devices

When a device has been connected to a central platform or solution, we usually operate with a central representation of that device. This is called a digital twin or a digital shadow depending on vendor. The idea is that the centralized system keeps track of the device's current state and its target state. This is the way that devices are typically managed.

Consider a signal that can take the values of red, yellow, and green. The digital shadow may report that it is currently green. A central solution may wish it to be red and set the digital twin target state to red. This is then sent to the device which updates the signal to red. The central solution has to exchange data with the device in order for this to happen.

The data received from the device is referred to as telemetry data. The word is made up from the Greek words *tele* meaning remote and *metron* meaning measurement; basically it means remote measurement. This measurement can have many different formats, and frequently it is encoded in some proprietary protocol that is unintelligible. Sometimes the readings are in a machine format that needs interpretation to make sense; sometimes it is encrypted. Data from devices is difficult to work with in its raw format.

The emerging standard for communicating with devices is the MQTT protocol. This was initially invented by IBM. It is a lightweight protocol that makes use of a Publish-Subscribe pattern. This means that certain information, like device readings, are published on a topic. Clients can subscribe to this topic and receive the information. The MQTT protocol is a layer 7 protocol built on top of the TCP/IP protocol (see Chapter 2). Remember that TCP was a protocol used at the transport layer (layer 4). The good thing about the TCP/IP system is that it is secure and reliable. It makes sure that all data packets are received and accounted for. It is the basis of the Internet and therefore widespread. In fact, AWS only accepts devices that use the TCP protocol, and pundits will sing the praises of the MQTT protocol as the standard of IoT. But such sweeping statements should be moderated since a large chunk of IoT devices actually don't employ the MQTT protocol or even the TCP protocol.

Many devices use UDP (see Chapter 2). It has a much simpler connection model and does not provide the handshake that TCP does. This means that UDP is considered less secure and more error-prone, since errors are not corrected by resending data packets as in TCP. The upside is that it has a much lower overhead and is faster. Time-sensitive applications that do not need to have the right order of packets and that can handle a little noise will therefore often employ UDP. For example, if you are continuously transmitting locations or a video feed, it may not be a big deal if a few location coordinates or a couple of frames are lost. You can easily reconstruct the route of the vehicle and follow the video still.

The challenges of protecting devices

On a sunny and warm Friday in October 2016, I was attending a conference at Princeton University where all the major experts on IoT and cybersecurity convened for a conference on IoT security. In the lunch break, word started spreading about what was happening with the Internet. Some said that a major botnet attack was going on. The irony of the situation was that during the IoT security conference, it turned out that the greatest IoT security event ever, that is, the Dyn attack, took place – an attack using the inherent vulnerabilities in devices. Briefly here is what happened:

Around noon, Dyn was the target of a Distributed Denial-of-Service (DDoS) attack that affected the entire Internet in Europe and North America. The effect was that major Internet platforms like Amazon, Netflix, Twitter, and PayPal became unavailable. Dyn is one of the companies that host the Internet's Domain Name Servers. The Domain Name System (see Chapter 2), which resolves domain names like wikipedia.org to IP addresses, was experiencing 10–20 times the normal traffic, which exhausted the bandwidth of the servers. DDoS attacks have been known for a long time but usually stem from PCs infected with malicious code. This code is something that can contact endpoints on the Internet. The trick here is that if you have thousands of computers doing this at the same time, then the web servers will become unresponsive because they cannot handle the amount of requests sent to them.

The software on the infected computer is controlled by some botnet owner. The reason it is called botnet is that the computers act as a network of robots that do what the owner asks them to do. The botnet type used in the Dyn attack is called Mirai. It specifically targets devices like security cameras, baby monitors, and printer. The Mirai code scans the Internet for devices and uses a list of more than 60 standard factory usernames and passwords to log in to the operating system and install a copy of itself on the device. As can be seen from this, the source of the vulnerability is standard credentials used by manufacturers. In the Dyn attack, more than 100,000 devices were used. While that seems like a lot of devices, it is not when we compare it to the total number of devices on the Internet, which is in the billions range already. Imagine if 100,000 devices can take down the Internet what a million or a billion can do.

More and more companies and cities are employing a Chief Information Security Officer (CISO) to be responsible for having adequate policies and standard operating procedures in place. A huge part of his or her job is to gain control of the sprawling array of devices being used. The number of devices is increasing fast, but today this area is the wild west of IT. Whereas earlier the Internet used to be a wild and unregulated place, this is not the case to the same extent anymore. For example, today no one would deploy thousands of web servers on the Internet with the same standard username and password like "admin" and "root." But this happens for devices as could be learned in abundance from the Mirai botnet's success. There are many reasons why devices are so unmanageable.

- **Difficult to interact with** – Devices are small, so they simply don't fit the same hardware that a computer does even though it gets better. Typically, it is difficult to interact with devices. They don't have a nice graphical user interface like a computer or smartphone, but have to be reached through some console or through other equipment. When they do come with APIs, these are often APIs that offer data in a proprietary format of the vendor and only the vendor's tools can interface with them. Even the largest device manufacturers are struggling with supplying proper APIs to get data from their solutions.

- **Low-cost production** – Most devices are produced on a market where low cost is the most important property. Security measures always add to the cost, and setting up systems and processes takes time and effort. Moreover, security usually makes deployment and usability harder. The basic competitive landscape therefore drives the market toward less security as it is now.

- **Lack of device vendor focus on security** – For device vendors it is rare that the company even has a CISO. We can only speculate as to what the precise reason for this is, but clearly there is not sufficient pressure from customers. If there were a big wish from customers for secure devices, the vendors would have had more focus. If you compare this situation to the big cloud vendors, there is a big difference. These vendors are dealing with experienced IT staff who know all the basics of security from their enterprise applications, and this security is a major driver in the adoption of cloud solutions.

- **Development inertia** – Traditionally devices have been deployed within a closed network that could not easily be accessed without physical control. This does not call for high security measures. Developers may keep developing devices as if they are in a closed circuit because they have been conditioned to do so back in the days of CCTV surveillance solutions. In this context, a standard administrator user with default password makes sense because a repair man, who would be the only one ever tinkering with the operating system, would easily be able to work with the device. The device in this standard scenario is protected by physical proximity and network segmentation.

- **Scale** – Every device is like a small computer and needs to be managed as such. When you have thousands, this becomes a problem only exacerbated by the preceding factors. It becomes necessary to build elaborate systems to keep track of each individual device and how it can be accessed securely.

All of these factors can and should be improved. Cities are in a unique position to drive this. As mentioned previously, the primary reason for the current situation is that governance is weak. A key initiative would therefore be to develop and adopt a robust set of practices to improve the shortcomings of the current device market. This can put some pressure on the ecosystem of vendors and implementation partners. Standards need to exist for many different areas, and they need to be developed by different stakeholder groups. This is part of the challenge that we were facing in New York City too. The approach we took was to initiate an interagency effort to develop and adapt existing standards for the new world of IoT.

Developing device standards: An interagency effort

Ubiquitous devices recording every aspect of our lives typically raise serious concerns from citizens. These need to be addressed, and the best way is to develop and enforce standards for how to approach important aspects. Privacy and security are big ones, but retention and architecture are other aspects worthy of note. These standards are interagency efforts, since different agencies know about and are concerned with different parts of the puzzle. The CISO is concerned mainly with the security of the solution and not necessarily the technological fit or maintainability. This is the concern of the IT organization, but they may not know or care about the functional adequacy of solutions. In order to develop sound and robust standards, it is necessary to engage different agencies.

Security standards

Security is one of the terms that are deceptively simple. "Do you want some more security or less security?" "Well, yes of course!" But what does that actually mean? It is not a substance like money that you can just increase or decrease. It is also not a Boolean concept that can be true or not. More than once have I heard someone claim: "and it is secure" as if that meant there would never be anything to worry about. A third classic misconception of security is that it is something that is handled with security technology as if it was a protective coating you can apply at the finish of your solution.

The first step toward more secure smart city solutions is to accept that security is not just one thing. It is a complex web of processes, technologies, and people. Standards are important in order to inform people about what to do, since it is too much to expect every one developing solutions to be on top of what makes for good security.

Types of security risks

Classical security thinking divides security into three aspects that need to be handled:

> **Confidentiality** is the ability to protect the data in such a way that only authorized people will be able to access it. According to the Federal Information Security Management Act of 2002 (FISMA), it is defined as "Preserving authorized restrictions on information access and disclosure, including means for protecting personal privacy and proprietary information...." A loss of confidentiality is therefore the unauthorized disclosure of information. In 2017 the credit rating agency Equifax was breached, and sensitive information about 146 million people's financial situation was stolen. This was a breach of confidentiality. While this was a classical hack of a web site, it could also involve devices and in different ways. In November 2017, fitness tracker Strava released a global heat map of athletic activity. This seems like a fairly innocuous marketing stunt since no one could identify any individual in isolation. However, they failed to realize that US Army soldiers deployed on secret bases were using the app, thereby giving away the confidentiality of the location of these bases through the activity patterns exposed by Strava.

Integrity means that the data is kept in its proper form and not tampered with or accidentally changed or damaged in any form. FISMA defines it thus: "Guarding against improper information modification or destruction, and includes ensuring information non-repudiation and authenticity...." A loss of integrity is the unauthorized modification or destruction of information. In 2010 hackers used the Stuxnet worm to infiltrate Iran's nuclear program, more specifically the centrifuges made for creating nuclear material. Stuxnet works by faking signals to control the centrifuges. By compromising the integrity of the data from sensors the centrifuges malfunctioned.

Availability refers to the extent to which data can be accessed and not just suddenly disappear. It is defined as "Ensuring timely and reliable access to and use of information..." (FISMA). A loss of availability is the disruption of access to or use of information or an information system. This was what happened with the WannaCry ransomware attacks. In this case, the virus infects the affected computers and encrypts the file drives. Entire networks had all their files encrypted, rendering them unavailable until a ransom was paid to the perpetrator who would then make the files available again.

Mitigation tactics

These are different types of security risks that smart city solutions face. The following are typical topics that need to be addressed in IoT security standards to that end:

- **Identity and access management** – Just like regular information systems, access to devices needs to be managed. While the general principles are the same, the technologies and solutions are typically very different. Also choices are many, so the standards need to address particular choices of technologies.

- **Cryptography** – When and how should data be encrypted? Is it just data in transit or also at rest? And how should it be done? Since cryptography carries with it its own problems, such as processing and development overhead and the risk of losing the cryptographic key, it is not trivial just to request all data to be encrypted at all times. The standard should also specify under what conditions encryption should be used. In general, only sensitive data need to be encrypted.

- **Incident management** – If an incident occurs, it is necessary to be able to detect it and mitigate attacks quickly. One of the reasons devices are a particular vulnerability is that breaches are not always detected. Furthermore, it might be necessary to inform the public about this.

- **Device management** – How are devices managed from an administration point of view? Far too often devices cannot be reached by the city itself even though they have bought and paid for the solution. Sometimes the devices cannot be reached for updates and patches at all. Sometimes a vendor does this. Standards should be put in place to specify how the lifecycle of a device should be managed, in order to keep it from being compromised by malware. For an overview of how different techniques impact different security features see Table 3-2.

Table 3-2. *Topics to address security risks*

	Confidentiality	Integrity	Availability
IAM	X		
Cryptography	X	X	
Incident management			X
Device management	X	X	X

There are no security standards directed toward the devices and IoT in particular, but the "FIPS 199, Standards for Security Categorization of Federal Information and Information Systems" is a good reference for the basics of assessing the risk connected with the data produced and handled by devices. The "NIST SP 800-53 Security and Privacy Controls for Federal Information Systems and Organizations" is a good source for security controls for information systems. It is also not specifically targeted at IoT and devices but a helpful resource.

Privacy standards

Devices pose new challenges for privacy. One classic concern is that the government is able to do surveillance of its citizens. Devices provide novel ways that this can happen. Cameras can run facial recognition algorithms to track people. Wireless routers can track cell phones, and wearables will tell where their owner is at any given time. All of these properties of devices come with great opportunities but also great risks if the residents of the city are not adequately protected from malicious use of this data.

The International Organization for Standardization (ISO) is currently in the process of creating a standard for privacy by design called the ISO/PC 317. Its goal is to build privacy into technology from the beginning. This directly addresses the current issues in many devices. The IEEE is developing a standard for communication between devices where users will be able to control the sharing of information. The Online Trust Alliance is an initiative of the Internet Society, and they have published an IoT Security and Privacy Trust Framework that sets forth standards which will be the foundation of future certification programs.

These initiatives show great activity in the area of privacy and IoT which cities can latch on to. It is too early to say which ones will be the most widespread, but it is safe to say that IoT privacy is something that is picking up steam right now. These are important sources of inspiration for privacy standards that cities can consult.

Architecture standards

IoT architecture is not a well-established discipline, and it is also developing in a fierce tempo. This fact along with the fragmented nature of existing standards makes it harder to develop actual standards for a city to use in its smart city initiatives. It may be counterproductive to aspire to develop the perfect standard that defines all the preferred technologies, since these change almost by the day. Rather it could be worthwhile to focus on key components that a standard should address.

Devices – What is considered a device? Even this seemingly simple question differs. Are devices just sensors of different sorts? Or are devices more colloquially understood like cell phones, tablets, and watches included? These may more closely resemble computers in many respects than sensors and actuators. This is an important consideration that will affect solutions.

Architectural layers – In IoT as in other types of computing, it may be preferred to have a specific set of layers that serve different functions. Some prefer a simple three-layer structure, but with the use of gateways at different levels, there may be more than just the three layers to take into consideration.

Integration – Defining the preferred method to interface with devices is an important thing to consider. This defines the ways that data is exchanged. First, it is necessary to consider the different integration patterns, like when to use Publish-Subscribe and Request-Response. Then consideration should be given to streaming or batch modes. Finally, preferred protocols need to be considered as well.

Connectivity – How should devices be connected? It could be through wifi, LTE, or some other radio technology. There could and probably should be multiple options, and thought should be given to the tradeoffs these different technologies provide, such as range, power, bandwidth, and cost. It is important to have guidelines on when to use these different options in order to optimize smart city implementations.

Platforms – Is there a preferred IoT platform? This may be helpful in developing a standardized way of handling IoT solutions. The IoT platform market is a particularly overcrowded and fragmented one. Since IoT reaches into many different domains, it may be difficult to find one platform that handles all aspects equally well. There could be different platforms in play, which makes it important to decide what to use them for.

Technologies – What are the preferred technologies? In IoT there are often multiple different options. It is a good idea to decide on preferred ones, because they need to be maintained and skills should be built around these preferred technologies. There are a great many protocols and programming languages out there, and it can seem like a jungle, but there are emerging standards that can be used.

Data – Where does the data from the IoT solution go? Is there a common Data Lake that should be used for sensor data? It could be important to maintain a centralized repository for device data. This would make it possible to leverage insights across different domains and build new services and products.

There are already a great number of different architecture standards available. As a matter of fact, there are so many that IEEE developed a standard to extract the best parts of other existing standards. The most important global standards are the following.

The IEEE P2413 is a Standard for an Architectural Framework for the Internet of Things. The purpose is to drive platform unification by increasing system compatibility and interoperability. This will help reduce the current industry fragmentation. Another key objective is to develop a reference architecture that will increase the transparency of IoT systems. It considers IoT as a three-tiered architecture with sensing, networking, and data communications and applications as the layers.

ETSI produces globally applicable standards for IT and communication technologies. The standard focuses on machine-to-machine communication and goes into some detail about specifying the different components, like gateways, network, and management functions.

The ITU is the United Nations' agency for information and communication technology. The particular focus of this organization is to improve access for people and communities that are currently underserved. Their approach is to focus on the ubiquity of technology. They categorize different types of devices:

- **Tagging things** – Are RFID devices. These are historically the oldest types of IoT devices.

- **Feeling things** – Are the sensors that measure signals from the environment.

- **Thinking things** – Are things that somehow act intelligently and autonomously to stimuli.

- **Shrinking things** – Are nanotechnologies that produce devices at nanoscale.

These suffice to show that many organizations have an interest in devices and the Internet of Things. A challenge will be to bring together the special interests of standardization organizations to converge on a "standard of standards."

Solution spotlights

Cities Coalition for Digital Rights

Cities Coalition for Digital Rights is a joint initiative between New York City, Amsterdam, and Barcelona and more than 20 other cities representing more than 100 million people to protect residents and visitors' digital rights. This is the first initiative in which cities have come together to protect digital rights on the global level. It is done in cooperation with the United Nations and focuses on privacy and data protection among other things. People should have the right not to be monitored and their data sold without consent. Their charter defines five headlines:

1) **Universal and equal access to the Internet and digital literacy** – Everyone should have access to affordable Internet and digital services on equal terms and have the skills to use them.

2) **Privacy, data protection, and security** – Everyone should expect privacy and have control of how their personal information is used and by whom for what purposes.

3) **Transparency, accountability, and nondiscrimination of data, content, and algorithms** – Any sort of potential bias in automated decisions should be transparent and open.

4) **Participatory democracy, diversity, and inclusion** – The Internet should be offered to anyone in order for them to participate in democratic processes no matter what device they have.

5) **Open and ethical digital service standards** – People should be able to use devices of their choice and expect interoperability. This means that cities should define their own open standards rather than let vendors use proprietary technologies to lock out residents who are not customers.

This is a supranational effort to build the interagency standards needed. These are focused on a subset of the necessary standards but are a good place to start.

Array of things

The University of Chicago, Argonne National Laboratory, and other universities have been working with the city of Chicago on a project to produce a system to support research into smart communities. The purpose is to provide (1) high spatial-temporal resolution measurements of the urban environment (air quality, noise, weather), (2) rapid deployment and test of new edge technologies, and (3) research and development by programmable devices. The project received a research grant from the US National Science Foundation to support its work in 2015. The Array of Things (AoT) has developed a node with multiple sensors and edge computing functionality. It builds on the Waggle platform, which is an open source hardware/software platform for deployment of sensor instruments with simple scripts for adding sensors and building a data pipeline. With this modular design, it is easy to add a new sensor instrument to the edge processor. The sensors connect through the edge computer and send data back to a central database. From here the data is published to a web server, and the readings can be used by anyone.

Concerns for privacy halted the rollout of the AoT nodes for a couple of years because residents of Chicago, where they were to be rolled out, were concerned that they would be tracked. Efforts were made to ensure the city and its public that this was not the case, but the privacy concerns seriously delayed the project.

There are now 200 nodes deployed that give insights into the air quality, noise, and traffic in Chicago. This data has been used for heat mitigation, traffic and pedestrian counts, prediction and detection of flooding, as well as efforts to predict the air quality in small 1×1 km cells. This project proves the power of city and university collaboration and has provided an open source platform that other cities can use to tackle similar challenges.

PlowNYC

A frequent problem and cause for complaints for residents of major cities is the failure to remove snow during and after snow falls. In New York City, the PlowNYC service was developed to let residents monitor in real time where snow plows were.

The plows are fitted with a GPS device and an LTE connection that constantly sends location data to a central service. But because cities like New York have a lot of buildings and other sources of noise, this signal is very noisy (as anyone will know who has tried to use their phone to find out where they are on the streets of Manhattan). Frequently, a vehicle will show up with coordinates in the center of a building, and an impossible trajectory appears when sampled locations are stitched together to track the route of the vehicle. The sensor data therefore has to be cleaned. This is a technique known as snap-to-grid. It is done by a back-end system that infers route based on previous readings and knowledge about the map of the city.

This solution initially produced some controversy and pushback from unions since their drivers' whereabouts could be monitored in real time. In order to mitigate this, the PlowNYC service only updates every 30 minutes even though data is available to do it real time. This is a good case to show how simple tracking of vehicles can give insight and transparency to a concern for city residents, but also why privacy concerns can impact a solution.

Exteros

This New York startup has developed a device that can count and categorize people, for example, in a shopping mall. It uses computer vision and artificial intelligence to categorize and count people as they move through the field of vision. The device is based on a Raspberry Pi, a camera, and a 3D printed case. This is a great example of the flexibility and availability of components to make innovative IoT solutions today. Earlier a vendor would have had to find an adequate camera and microcontroller. Then the logic would have had to be developed. In this case, machine learning models need to be trained and implemented on the chip. Then a case manufacturer would have to be found, and finally an assembly line would need to be set up to assemble and test each device. Now, this can be done literally from your bedroom. This is an important learning point for cities as well as startups and hobbyists: components for effective and innovative solutions are already available to everyone and relatively inexpensive.

Summary

Devices can be grouped into three types: sensors, actuators, and processors or a combination of those. Sensors measure something like particles in the air, temperature, or movement, actuators act on the environment like opening and closing a gauge or a door, and processors process data. These come in many different forms with different characteristics in terms of their ability to be adapted to new functions, processing capability, and energy consumption. The three main types of processors are computer, microcontroller, and integrated circuits.

Working with devices in a city context is challenging because the skills in the technology units are typically not generalizable to IoT. Devices also do not provide the same possibility for management as traditional IT systems with clearly defined service windows and rollback options. Devices are always on and difficult to upgrade and patch, which is why they are rarely if ever maintained.

Communicating with a device from an IoT platform is necessary in most cases and has its own challenges as the sheer number of devices makes it hard to scale. Connecting hundreds of thousands of devices manually to an IoT platform is simply not feasible. There are different protocols for communicating with devices which adds to the challenge of building IoT solutions with multiple devices. Another even more daunting challenge is protecting these devices, which the Dyn attack in October 2016 from connected devices showed. This incident took down large portions of the Internet half a day. There are many reasons for devices being a weak point in city and Internet infrastructure. Some of them include difficulty maintaining devices, lack of focus on security by vendors, development inertia, and scale.

Making sure the city has the right standards is one way to minimize the challenges with the current ad hoc style of implementation. These standards should include security, privacy, and architecture standards. Having these in place and enforcing them will help make smart city solutions more sustainable and secure.

CHAPTER 4

Data

The modern city runs on data. For example, collecting the right taxes is crucial to city revenue, without which city services would not be funded and cease to work. Registering who needs to pay what and when in taxes is a data problem. Making sure that residents receive the right social and health services is a data problem. We need to know who lives where and what their needs are. If this does not work, people will live in poverty and potentially die due to lack of medical attention. Monitoring air quality and water quality is also a data problem because it depends crucially on a city's ability to collect, store, and access data. In its simplest form, this is what we need to focus on (see Figure 4-1).

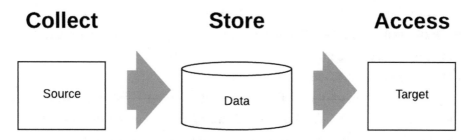

Collect **Store** **Access**

Figure 4-1. *Data management*

However, this is where the simplicity stops. Data is not just out there like trash that you can collect and take to the junk yard. It can be difficult to get to it, and when you do get to it, it can be difficult to make sense of it. Even then more issues surround data, like regulatory requirements,

© Anders Lisdorf 2020
A. Lisdorf, *Demystifying Smart Cities*, https://doi.org/10.1007/978-1-4842-5377-9_4

ownership, and the structure of data. There are multiple forces that affect how a city can use data (see Figure 4-2).

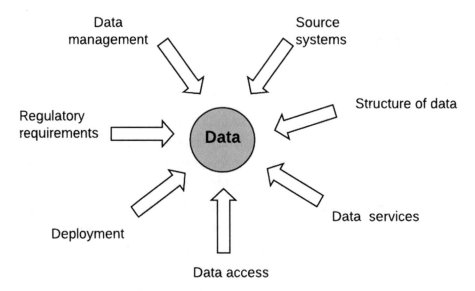

Figure 4-2. *Forces affecting the use of data*

For each use case, the power and nature of that force varies. For example, not all types of data have any regulatory requirements or have to have any data management, but all data has a structure and needs to be deployed in a solution somewhere.

In this chapter, we will look at each of these forces that shape the use of data in the city. We will look at the different types of source systems where we find city data, what structure it has, what data services technologies we use to manage it, how data can be accessed by users and other systems, how it can be deployed as running solutions, the regulatory requirements around data, and how data is managed in terms of governance and quality processes.

Source systems

Looking at the potential sources of data is a good place to start. Data is always created by a system somehow, but the process and nature of that system has an impact on the data and how it needs to be integrated, stored, and managed.

Systems of record

A system of record is a system that serves as the authoritative source of information for its particular type of information. An example could be a payroll system, which serves as the authoritative source of who gets what in salary at what time and why. A system of record is used to manage business processes that the city is responsible for like social services, education, permits, HR, taxes, and so on. These are the backbone of the city and determine how it runs and are often also characterized as mission-critical applications because they need to run in order for the city to work. If a payroll system is down, it better be up and running smoothly come pay day; otherwise, city employees will go home, and important city functions will shut down.

The importance of these systems from a data perspective is tied to the character of their data as authoritative. While other systems may contain similar or derived data, systems of record are masters of data and always take preference to other sources of data – not necessarily for all data though. Let us take the example of a building permit system. If a company wants to build on a site, they need to submit an application. This will as a minimum contain the address of the site and the registration number of the company. While the building permit system is authoritative for the application process and result, it is not authoritative for the address data or the company registration data. The existence of a company will typically be registered in one system and the address of the building site in another system. If someone decides to use the company registration data for a report, for example, and they take it from the building permit system, it is derivative and in general is not recommended. One reason is that changes to the company in the proper system of record may not be reflected in the building permit system. There could also be regulatory restrictions on the data that only the proper source system is aware of, such as privacy. It could be that a person has asked for her name or address to be corrected or deleted. According to the European General Data Protection Regulation (GDPR), this needs to be enforced in all systems. We will return to the issue of regulatory data later.

This is why it is always important to determine what systems of record are masters for the types of data we are working with. If we need building permits, we need to find the right source. If we need company registration data, we need to identify the right source for that even if we already have it in the building permit system. It is not always easy or straightforward to identify the source system for a given piece of information. Sometimes it is even a political issue what system is the proper system of record for a given type of data, since certain agencies feel they own the data rather than another.

Sensors

Sensors are quite a different type of source. At an abstract level, you could say that a sensor converts some aspect of the physical environment (heat, air quality, sound) into an electrical signal which then is transmitted or stored as data. The first issue with sensor data is to get to it in the first place. Sometimes the sensor data is stored locally and needs to be physically retrieved as is the case with certain types of vehicle counting sensors. Other times the vendor manages an end-to-end solution where they will give you access to the end product but not the actual sensor data.

Even when you can get to the sensor data, it is rarely comprehensible without understanding how the sensor works, what it measures, and how it measures. Often the data format itself is in a proprietary format, and the readings are impossible to understand without context. This means that data needs to be translated in order to be intelligible. Consequently, sensor data typically has to pass through additional processing steps in order to be converted into something meaningful.

The next issue is that concepts that are intuitively meaningful to us when we talk about them break down when we get to the physical level of the sensor. In the case of air quality, it seems straightforward that good-quality air is clear and clean and bad-quality air is not. But what actually goes into good and bad air when we break it down? A common measure of air quality is the number of particles measured in PM (particulate matter). Already here we have to decide because there are two standard measures – PM10 and PM2.5. The number refers to the particle sizes in micrometer. While both tell something meaningful about the air quality, they have different health effects. PM2.5 particles are more dangerous from a health perspective.

However, this is just one aspect of air quality and says nothing about gasses like carbon monoxide, ozone, sulfur dioxide, and nitrogen dioxide. All of these in various degrees affect our health. Add to this that certain types of sensors like electrochemical sensors degrade over time, which means that the precision fluctuates. We end up in a situation where something we expect to be a straightforward sensor reading requires a lot of decisions and choices before we get to the data we really want.

Sensor data is challenging to work with but is critical for many smart city applications.

Online sources

The Internet is ubiquitous and naturally also a potential source of data in a smart city context. Not all web sites are equally interesting, but some are very useful.

Social networks play a large role in peoples' life and are consequently a rich source of data about the life in the city. Not all data is public, but some social networks have a more public purpose, such as Twitter, Instagram, and LinkedIn. These can in some circumstances be used as data sources. Twitter, for example, offers the Twitter Firehose. This is a service that lets you receive all tweets that match your criteria. An example could be all tweets within the city. This way a city can get all data on what residents and visitors are talking about at any given point in the city.

Another example of publicly available data is the Connected Citizens Program run by Waze. The Waze service monitors participants' route and speed through a city, which allows them to recommend optimal routes from one point to another. It also allows users to crowdsource important traffic events like accidents, roadwork, and congestion. This data is what the Connected Citizens Program offers participating cities access to. The data is published on a URL and updated frequently.

Other examples of publicly available data online are statistics, weather data, and so on. There are also data vendors and data marketplaces that allow you to buy even more data. Online data is a rich source. Working with online data sources is significantly easier than sensors since they all can be connected to with standardized methods.

Structure of data

Another way of looking at the data is to focus on the structure. While data is always stored in bits, there are many ways it can be encoded.
It is common to distinguish three kinds of data structure: structured, semi-structured, and unstructured.

There are different types of data that need to be handled in different ways by different types of storage solutions. Getting to know these different types is a good start.

Structured data

We find structured data in databases, Excel sheets, and other tabular formats. Tabular data is easy to spot, since this is basically data you can access and store in a table. Each row has a set of columns that define some characteristic of the record in the row. An example of tabular data would be a list of all government properties. Each row would be a property, and each column would be a piece of information about it like the address, year it was built, estimated value, and so on. The Excel sheet is a good tool for viewing and editing tabular data, but the more common format used in IT solutions is a comma-separated values (CSV) file. There are many other formats, but the basic structure of a row defining a record with a number of values in columns is the primitive form of tabular data that was used all the way back to the first mainframes. This is still very widely used across all different sectors. Structured data is what we use for reporting and is the most accessible type.

Semi-structured data

Where structured data can be immediately opened in a spreadsheet, this is not the case with semi-structured data. It is however potentially possible to extract the data and put it into a structured format. Semi-structured data has a greater variety of structure as it can contain tree-like structures. Sometimes the structure is defined in the data set itself with tags as is the case with HTML and JSON; other times it is defined in conjunction with the data as in XML. In both cases, the structure is self-contained in the file.

Semi-structured data is used frequently online and in general for data exchange because it is flexible and self-explanatory. In order to turn it into structured data, it has to be parsed based on the metadata contained in file.

Unstructured data

For unstructured data, it is not even in principle possible to bring it into a spreadsheet. It is not organized in any preset manner. It can be a blob of binary data as is the case with video or audio. It could be machine data where a continuous stream of readings are stored. In order to use and process unstructured data, it is not sufficient to parse it as is the case with semi-structured data. It is necessary to extract it based on algorithms. Consequently, there is a need to understand what the data is and what we are looking for in the data before we can extract any information.

Data services

In the past decade, we have seen an explosion in data services technologies. The past four decades have been dominated by the relational database as the default storage type, but under the guise of NoSQL and big data, other innovative solutions have come to the attention of data professionals. These data services have great variety, but all in one way or another manages storage of and access to data. They all have a specific focus aligned with a specific type of use case. In the following, we will look at a couple of the most popular types.

Object storage

This is a new type of storage popularized by AWS Simple Storage Service (or S3). The purpose of object storage is to provide a simple way to store and retrieve files regardless of their nature or format. It is used for logs, comma-separated files, video, audio, and so on. It does not have folders but rather is organized into buckets where the files are stored. If structure has to be imposed, it has to be through the file name. Consequently, some attention has to be given to naming the files.

It is accessed through a web service API that uses the standard HTTP protocol, and the file simply has a unique name and the binary data of the file. It is a versatile way of storing data that can be used in multiple settings. While AWS was the first to use it, all the major cloud vendors have a version of this today, but the S3 implementation has become the reference standard. Object storage is typically also the cheapest way to store data.

Relational databases

The relational database management system (RDBMS) revolutionized how we could store and retrieve data. Even though multiple other offerings exist today, the RDBMS is still popular. According to research from 2017 by Gartner group it accounted for 90% of all data management revenue.

The theories that form the basis of the modern relational database were developed by Edgar Frank Codd. His 1970 paper "Relational Completeness of Data Base Sublanguages" still today forms the basis for how relational databases are structured and how we interact with them.

The speed, flexibility, and efficiency with which you can store data in an RDBMS are significantly higher than storing data in files, which was the alternative before the 1970s. The RDBMS is built around tables that are predefined. In these tables, you input single transactions, called records. These are comparable to lines in an Excel sheet, and the table equals the columns.

However, these were all features that exist for files as well. The difference is that around these tables logic exists in the RDBMS to tie together different tables through keys and also to maintain consistency between different tables. With the RDBMS came the now ubiquitous Structure Query Language or SQL. This is now a de facto standard that is employed even in modern databases that are not relational and used every day by millions of business analysts and data professionals alike. SQL is a simple declarative language that lets you access specific records or subset of records based on filters and transformations that you want to employ.

A company like Oracle was an early leader in this technology and later diversified into other areas. In the last couple of decades, functional equivalents have been developed in the open source community: MySQL and PostgreSQL are the major ones that have millions of deployments. These also form the basis of some of the cloud vendors' RDBMS offerings. Since they are compliant with standard SQL, they are easy to switch to for most people who have been used to traditional RDBMS.

Document database

Where relational databases store the data in tabular form in preexisting schemas, document databases are not constrained in the same way. The fundamental storage unit is the document. MongoDB was the early open source leader in this space and has effectively been driving much of the development. They are built to work with JSON documents, which are semi-structured text, but they have evolved significantly since then, and some of the functionality associated with the RDBMS has been built into them. An important difference is that the document database will take any data with any structure, whereas the RDBMS needs the data to comply with a preexisting schema. This is another versatile data store that will often be used by applications where the structure may change frequently.

Key value stores

Key value stores are the simplest type of data store available. It simply has a key and associated data. Here the key needs to include all the indexing logic you could want. The databases typically have indexing functionality to locate keys or search for ranges in keys. Another difference from object stores is that the values can be arrays, that is, multiple values and not just one file. Also many key value stores have a limit on the size of data per record, which is not the case for object storage.

This is one of the fastest-growing types of data store because of its flexibility, scalability, and high throughput. There are different flavors depending on the typical workload. If you work with simple pairs of values, you might want one type, but if you want to be able to input multiple values in an array, it is another one. In general the key-value databases are optimized for specific use cases where they outperform competition from the RDBMS, but not very convenient outside their narrow focus. They are not general purpose or easy to manage. Almost all logic has to be handled in application code. They are also not SQL compliant, so analysts used to getting the data they need from the source will have difficulty.

Graph databases

A graph in this context is not the visualization in the monthly sales report. It should be understood along the lines of discrete mathematics where a graph is a set of discrete vertices connected by edges, that is, in more common terms, a network. This means that the basic structure is defined by how a record is connected to other records. Similar to other databases, information about the record can be stored, but the difference is that the relations are the primary focus. This type of database has also been around for decades but only recently come into focus due to open source efforts like Neo4J. It is well suited to problems that have a network structure to them since it is optimized for identifying relationships between observations like social networks, criminal investigations, fraud detection, and so on.

Block chain

The block chain is actually also a way of storing data. It operates with a so-called distributed ledger, which means that everyone has the same ledger and operates on it. The same could in principle be done with a file that everyone shared, but the block chain has been optimized for synchronizing data between copies and doing it in a format that makes it impossible to alter afterward. This is called non-repudiation in technical terms and refers to the possibility of proving transactions. This is a key property which no other storage technology does as well. In a database, you can always go and change a data entry, similarly with a file. If everybody works on the same shared data source, how can we determine which version is correct? This is a particularly prominent problem when it comes to transactions of property. This is being done today of course by banks, but it requires an elaborate system to clear that a transaction is correct and make it official. Once a transaction has been stored in the distributed ledger, it can no longer be disputed or reversed in any way, and it is free and open for anyone to see that it has been done. This is why block chain is good for problems where trust and validating data is an issue. As a general storage option, it has serious drawbacks because it is very slow. From the time a transaction is made until it is validated by the block chain, it can take minutes. For the original Bitcoin block chain, it was around 10 minutes. Other block chains have been developed that are faster, but it will never be able to compete with any other storage technology in terms of latency. It is also very costly in terms of processing, since all nodes in the distributed ledger need to process everything and generate new blocks.

For an over view of pros and cons of different data storage technologies see table 4-1.

Table 4-1. *Pros and cons for data storage options*

Technology	Pro	Con	Ideal Use
Object storage	Cheap storage, simple, scalable	Difficult to search and query	Large unstructured files like pictures, video, and sound
RDBMS	Flexible, multipurpose, easy to query, quick to develop new solutions	Not good for massive amounts of data; schemas need to be defined in advance	Reporting, transactions, applications
Document database	Scalable, no schema definition needed, low latency	Not good for analytical queries	Storing messages
Key value store	Low latency even with very large amounts of data, highly scalable	Not flexible, requires a lot of development work	Transactions, measurements, managing online sessions
Graph databases	Good for discovery problems	Addresses only limited set of use cases	Discovery of relationships between entities
Block chain	Distributed and not centralized, not possible to tamper with recorded data	Very high latency, not scalable, and limited in types of data	Data that can be disputed

Data access

Data stored in a database is not very valuable if it is not being used. This is why data access is a key consideration. In some cases, the pattern is that data is accessed by another system in which case we call it machine-to-machine or M2M. The other pattern is where human end users access the data in a graphical user interface.

Machine-to-machine

Perhaps the most frequent form of access to data is from one system to another. This is the realm of data integration. The data integration market is expected to grow to almost $25 billion by 2027 according to market analytics firm Stratistics MRC. This is an area of great investment and focus from vendors and customers alike. There are different ways for this to happen. In this context, we will just look at a selection.

Web services – One of the most dominant forms of M2M access is the web service, since it offers great flexibility in design and usage. The web service typically comes with a description of what data it has and how it can be accessed. There are a number of functions that can be called that will return the data based on input parameters. With web services, distributed systems can be made at scale, and devices can communicate seamlessly with each other. If it is necessary to offer data to both external and internal systems, it is a well-suited solution since API management portals can manage everything from security and registering new users to limiting number of calls or data volume.

FTP – FTP is a way to move files between file shares across the Internet. It is one of the solid workhorses of today's M2M solutions, since it is a simple way to perform the simple task of moving a file. There are multiple free open source tools, but also commercial managed file transfer solutions. These are usually employed when more advanced features like guaranteed delivery, authentication, and receipt of notifications are used.

They are especially valuable for trusted communication with external parties and are used, for example, for sending evidence to attorneys or health records to hospitals.

ODBC – While web services are often focused on individual records and FTP on pre-generated files, the need for a more flexible access to bulk data is increasing. ODBC is one way to offer tailored access to data in a database. Instead of developing a process that will generate a file every time a new need arises, either direct access to the tables or a view can be built tailored to the specific needs of each particular consumer. Once the view on the data has been generated, nothing more needs to be done. When the consumer queries the data, it will be up to date because the query is a view on top of the master data sources. This is convenient when many different consumers need different access to the data. Rather than generating multiple partially duplicate files, views can be configured. The caveat with ODBC is always that it can impact the performance of the database if queries are complex.

Graphical user interface

Every day millions of managers, business analysts, and operational staff need access to data in one form or another in order to perform their job adequately. The graphical user interface is how this is made possible. It has to make it possible for users to find and use the data they need.

Data portal – One way of accessing data is through a portal, which is nothing more than a platform that gives access to files or views of data. One popular form of data portal is the open data portal that many cities have. There are different tools, both commercial and open source, but they all work on precompiled files that are being exposed to end users for download or browsing in a tabular format on the platform. It is usually possible to search for descriptions and tags in order to find the data. The data portals are typically used for external users.

Business intelligence – The business intelligence (BI) tools have been a mainstay of reporting for decades already. These are being used internally and also run on prepared data. But BI tools usually connect to a Data Warehouse, which is a relational database, where data has been optimized for particular reporting needs. Today the end user often has a great degree of flexibility in how data can be viewed and filtered in the BI tool.

Web sites – Public web sites are another way to publish data. In this case, it is most often in a fixed format where all details about the visualization have been made. The same degree of flexibility that a BI tool offers is not available. This will often be authoritative data published for the sake of transparency or information. The difference compared to a data portal and BI tools is that everyone should be able to access and understand the data, since it just requires that you go to the URL.

Deployment

Data needs to be stored, and a plethora of technologies exist. Especially in the last decade, we have seen an explosion in new types of storage with colorful names that may be difficult to understand. One aspect that cuts across the different technologies is whether they run on premise in the city's own data center or in the cloud in a vendor's data center. It is often possible to get the same technologies in both forms of deployment. Let us start by looking at what the differences are between these.

On premise

Until recently, the default choice was to store data in an internal data center that the organization owned and operated. This has many advantages since you control physical access to the data and define all aspects of the networks. It also has some drawbacks since you need to have staff that can maintain and develop the infrastructure. An on-premise infrastructure has to take care of the following:

- **Physical site** – Which has to be managed and maintained. Functions like cooling, fire suppression mechanisms, and physical access control have to be taken care of. Furthermore, multiple sites have to be maintained for resilience purposes.

- **Physical servers** – The physical machines have to be ordered, unwrapped, connected, switched, and decommissioned safely at end of life.

- **Storage** – It is necessary to set up solutions that can serve archiving and backup functionality. Often storage on shared drives is also set up for employees to use. This has to be configured and maintained.

- **Networks** – The physical network connects the servers and creates the structure of how data flows. Firewalls, network segmentation, failover, and disaster recovery have to be planned for across the different sites in the data center.

- **Operating systems** – On the server, operating systems have to be installed before they can be used for anything sensible. They have to be maintained, upgraded, and patched in order to remain functional and secure.

- **Virtualization** – Today most servers running applications on premise are virtualized. This means that they can be moved from one physical server to another. This is a layer that requires expertise and configuration as well.

All of the things in the preceding text require dedicated specialists and units to handle as well as standard operating procedures and support organizations. It offers a high degree of control.

The perception is that on premise is safer than cloud deployments. In terms of confidentiality, you are able to maintain a perimeter around your data. With a firewall and other networking technologies, you can decide who can get access to what. Once you are on a network, you can easily connect to other solutions and data on the network, but no one on the outside will be able to access your network unless you allow it through the firewall. But security is more than just keeping the data confidential; you also have to protect it against data loss, so solutions for backup and recovery have to be set up and maintained. Furthermore, a firewall is only as good as the weakest link, so if there is one hole, potentially the whole network could be compromised.

Scaling and maintaining an on-premise data center also requires resources and takes time. If someone needs a server for something, it has to be ordered and set up. Equipment must be bought in advance, which ties up funds.

On premise is a good option if you have something very special and nonstandard because you have the possibility to choose the exact hardware and software that fit your needs. You are also able to tailor configuration completely to your needs. It is also a benefit from a security perspective that you can completely cut off the data from the Internet if the default is that you work with sensitive data in one way or another. Maintaining a sufficient level of specialized resources can be a challenge though.

Cloud

In the past decade, the cloud has become an increasingly popular option. The cloud is strictly speaking nothing more than someone else running your data center. This also means that it is possible to make use of economies of scale. The cloud vendors do all the maintenance and development of the infrastructure, and customers pick only what they need. This has enabled customers to focus on areas where they want to have expertise, which in most cases is not running a data center.

When we are talking about the cloud, it is important to be precise, since there are many vendors and services out there. The American National Institute of Standards and Technology (NIST) has provided the most common definition of what is meant by cloud computing. The definition is as follows:

> *Cloud computing is a model for enabling ubiquitous, convenient, on-demand network access to a shared pool of configurable computing resources (e.g., networks, servers, storage, applications, and services) that can be rapidly provisioned and released with minimal management effort or service provider interaction.*[1]

There are five essential characteristics for something to be cloud:

1. **On-demand self-service** – The user has to be able to provision the resources needed without the intervention of the vendor or anyone else.

2. **Broad network access** – The service has to be accessible through standard interfaces like a computer, tablet, smartphone, and so on.

3. **Resource pooling** – The computer resources are pooled across multiple customers in a multi-tenant model. These are gathered in data centers that the consumer has no detailed influence on. For some services, it is possible to specify country and state though.

---

[1] *The NIST Definition of Cloud Computing*, Peter Mell, Timothy Grance

4. **Rapid elasticity** – Capabilities can be rapidly
   provisioned and de-provisioned depending on need
   and are able to scale rapidly often automatically
   with demand.

5. **Measured service** – The use and billing is metered
   at some appropriate level of abstraction, like hour,
   bandwidth, CPU usage, and number of users, to
   provide transparency, control, and monitoring.

While there are many ways that this can be implemented, they are
good indicators of what is unique about cloud computing. If you compare
with on premise, it is not on demand, not necessarily available anywhere
outside the internal network. It is not very elastic, since it is necessary to
order new servers if demand picks up. Another important point is that it is
not metered, but a lot of up-front investments must be done that are sunk
costs. This is why you often hear about a move from capital expenditure
to operational expenditure, when it comes to cloud computing. It is not
necessary to make capital investments in equipment before starting.

Another important point of the NIST definition is the division into
three types: Software as a Service (SaaS), Platform as a Service (PaaS), and
Infrastructure as a Service (IaaS).

- **Software as a Service** – Is the ability of the consumer
  to access system features through a standard interface
  like a web browser. The consumer has no control of
  the underlying infrastructure except for what can be
  configured in the application. The vendor provides
  and maintains all aspects of the product except for
  application-specific configurations. Well-known
  consumer-level examples are Gmail, Office 365,
  Salesforce, and Slack. An example of a SaaS storage
  technology is Google Docs or SharePoint Online.

- **Platform as a Service** – Is the capability to deploy to the cloud applications that are developed by the consumer. The consumer has no control of the underlying networks, operating systems, or storage, but has control of the applications that are developed. PaaS storage solutions are AWS S3, Google Cloud Spanner, and Snowflake Data Warehouse.

- **Infrastructure as a Service** – Provides the consumer with the capability to provision fundamental computing resources like storage, network, and processing. The consumer is able to install and run any type of software as if it were on private hardware. An example of IaaS data storage is block storage, which can be attached to a virtual machine for extending disk storage.

Comparison between on premise and cloud

As we saw previously, there are a number of different options for how to deploy data management and storage solutions. The cloud has to be divided into three subsections (see Table 4-2).

Table 4-2. *Who manages what on premise and in the cloud?*

On Premise	IaaS	PaaS	SaaS
Applications	Applications	Applications	Applications
Data	Data	Data	Data
Runtime	Runtime	Runtime	Runtime
Middleware	Middleware	Middleware	Middleware
Operating System	Operating System	Operating System	Operating System
Virtualization	Virtualization	Virtualization	Virtualization
Servers	Servers	Servers	Servers
Storage	Storage	Storage	Storage
Networking	Networking	Networking	Networking

White = customer manages, Grey = vendor manages

In relation to data, the most interesting layer is the database layer, since this is where the most important technologies for storing data are. At the infrastructure level, we also have storage. This is a lower level of disk storage. At the other end, we have SaaS solutions that are mostly used only for end user purposes and rarely for building more sophisticated solutions. Most choices will revolve around how to deploy databases.

There is no right or wrong, so if we look at the pros and cons, it will be easier to see in a given situation what is recommended (see Table 4-3 for details).

Table 4-3. *Pros and cons of different deployment options*

	On Premise	**IaaS**	**PaaS**	**SaaS**
Pros	Full control of hardware, established practices	No need for physical sites, High degree of control	No maintenance, High degree of resilience	No maintenance or development, Circumvents IT department, Industry best practice built into tool
Cons	Capital intensive, finding skilled resources is difficult	Maintenance is required, Resilience needs to be designed by customer	Need to develop and configure ad hoc solutions, Low possibility for correction	Very little control of solution performance, No possibility for correction
Typical deployments	Mission-critical solutions	Storage, virtual servers, migration of existing infrastructure	New custom applications	Noncritical business solutions with heavy end user interaction

This is just a general overview based on the current state of the market. The market is moving and the solutions offered are also developing. Therefore, it should not be taken as a fixed guideline.

Regulatory requirements

All data is not equal, and it is not necessarily free for us to build any solution with any data we might be able to find in a source system. Since data carries information about real-world people and impacts their lives, there are certain areas where special regulation applies. This data can be abused if it is not managed properly. We may be familiar with regulations of data in financial and pharmaceutical industries, but it also applies in cities. In this section, we will review some of the more widespread regulatory regimes that impact how data should be managed, which can have far-reaching consequences for the implementation of a solution and its risk profile since it can require additional processes or constraints.

Health data

Many countries have regulations that govern how health data can be used and how it needs to be protected. In the United States, the Health Insurance Portability and Accountability Act, or HIPAA, is a central regulatory scheme enacted in 1996 in order to modernize how healthcare information was used and shared. It imposes rules on how personally identifiable information (PII) should be protected in order to protect the individual. Specifically, it is Title II that regulates the protection of Protected Health Information (PHI), which is information related to treatment and payment for health services. The rule stipulates that use of personal data should be minimal, any use of it or breach is disclosed to the person involved, and it should be possible to get insight into the data stored as well as opportunity to correct it. In addition to this, there are rules for what processes and technical provisions must be in place to protect the data. HIPAA data requires some extra processes to protect and maintain. There are guidelines as to what precisely counts as HIPAA data and also certification processes for solutions handling HIPAA data.

In the European Union, similar legislation also exists, for example, the UK Data Protection Act of 1998, which implements many of the same provisions as HIPAA, like right to access of own health data and access only be granted to those who are responsible for the individual.

In general, health data is a type of data that requires additional processes for data management and protection, since the person involved needs to be kept informed and also has rights of access. This poses special challenges when health data needs to be used for solutions.

Criminal justice data

Another category of data that requires special attention is criminal justice data. This is information about a person's criminal record, summons, identity history, biometric data, and so on. This is typically guarded with the same care as health data but differs in important respects. In this case, not all data can be disclosed to the person in question, and there is (obviously) not the same possibility for correcting data.

In the United States, the Criminal Justice Information Services (CJIS) division of the FBI has developed a number of requirements for handling its data. CJIS data is data that helps law enforcement agencies enforce the law. This could be about case history, evidence, and a wide range of other types of data. If the criminal justice data in one particular solution has one component of CJIS, all data is considered CJIS data and needs to comply with these requirements. The requirements are far reaching and cover access to the data center, encryption, and authentication. There is no general certification for CJIS, so each separate solution has to be certified individually.

For criminal justice data, special attention has to be given to data access.

Personal data in general

Personally identifiable information (PII) is a more generic term that refers to data that can be uniquely related to a person. Different countries have different regulations for the general protection of this data. Outside of the European Union, it has not been commonplace to have any such protection. In China and the United States, large amounts of personal data are collected without any sort of regulations. With the General Data Protection Regulation (GDPR) of the European Union, the focus on personal data in and of itself has come to the center of attention.

Compared to the health and criminal justice types of data, PII is general and does not depend on context. The GDPR covers personal data and how it is managed. The individual has a right to know what information is stored and also to correct it. This was also possible in the healthcare context, but the new aspect here is that the individual now has a right to be forgotten. Unless other laws require a data processor to store the data, the individual can request all personal data to be deleted from all systems. The data processor has to demonstrate processes for this and keep track of the data deleted. Another provision is data minimization, that is, only storing the relevant data and restricting access only to authorized users, who have a good reason to see it.

While GDPR is a European Union regulation, it has a wider impact, since it covers all European citizens regardless of where their data is stored. This means that it is also in force in the United States. Consequently, any company anywhere in the world can be fined for infringements on the GDPR. This is why we see the impact of GDPR on a worldwide scale.

Handling personal data in general now requires a number of processes and protections that were only in place for specialized cases like health and criminal information. This requires us to reflect on when we need personal information.

Data management

We have to think about data as something we actively manage. It is not just something that is out there or something that comes to us automatically and plugs right into our smart city solutions. The discipline around the data is what we look at in this section. Data governance has to do with the decision processes and frameworks around data, master data management has to do with the operational processes, and data quality has to do with how to improve the integrity and consistency of the data.

Data governance

Just as other forms of governance, data governance has to do with policies, processes, and decisions. In data governance, we look for who has what authority to create, change, and view specific types of data.

For governance to work, we need someone to be responsible and make decisions. There will typically be a Chief Data Officer or CDO at the top. There will also be a governance board with key stakeholders.

First it needs to be determined at a general logical level what data exists and is of relevance to the organization. What are the key concepts that exist, like buildings, persons, payments, devices, and so on? Once this has been determined, the responsibility for each concept has to be delegated to an owner. The data owner is the one responsible for where the master source is, what the different entities are, and how they are defined. This will frequently be delegated to more operational people. The data owner does not need to have that precise title, but the responsibility has to be placed with someone in the organization for data governance to work.

One of the most common misconceptions is that data is an IT problem and should be handled by IT. This is a frequent reason data governance initiatives fail. It is seen as a technical fix that you can buy a solution for, but it is not. An IT organization does not have the domain knowledge and the understanding of the processes that produce and depend on the data.

Only the business units do that. Data governance is an agenda that cannot be driven from below. It needs to be implemented and prioritized from the top in order to be effective.

Master data management

Whereas governance is focused on the general principles and processes, master data management is focused on the tooling. It is usually done in conjunction with data governance. Master data is the authoritative source of a given piece of information. Information will often be used across multiple processes and solutions. This means that some data will be derivative. If we don't have a clear idea about who is the authoritative source of a piece of data, multiple versions of the truth may appear. This situation can impede real-world processes and functions. Think of the simple case of a person and his or her address. If the address is changed in one system but not in another system, suddenly we have two versions of the truth, which will create a problem when we want to contact that person maybe in an emergency. Do we use one address or the other? This is why we need to define what the authoritative master of different pieces of information is.

Conceptual model – At the top level is a conceptual model. This will typically have a few key entities. This will have a definition that should make sense to anyone with no background in the domain.

Logical model – The logical model goes into detail about how the entities are related and what the attributes of the entities are. It is still not tied to any physical implementation and could be implemented across multiple systems.

Physical model – The physical model consists of technical detail of the implementation of the data. This is what can be the basis of code to be implemented on a database. Here the keys and data types need to be defined.

With MDM you manage data across a number of different solutions working on the same data in order to bring consistency about data between solutions. This ensures that the organization works on the same data. There are different approaches to doing this. It might be done by synchronizing across solutions, bringing data from other solutions into one, establishing another independent database that collects from all systems, or creating a unified view based on data sources based on business rules.

Typical MDM solutions work from an established model of how data should be structured in a domain. If we take the example of the person domain, there should be information about address, social security number, phone number, citizenship, and so on. When multiple systems produce data about a person, they need to map their internal view of a person against this master version. Decisions have to be made about what happens when two systems have conflicting information about a person. Does the system update from the master or does it overwrite the master?

For data about persons, it is often the case that the name or address may be misspelled or spelled in an alternative way: is Johny Smith the same person as Johnny Smith?

Even when the names are identical, it can be a problem. It is not always easy to spot if Jane Smith in system A is the same as Jane Smith in system B, when there are 351 people with that name. This is why MDM has to deal with rules about matching. Sometimes clear rules can be made to match a person in one system to another, like having the same social security number. This is called deterministic matching.

However, it is not always the case that you have sufficient data to provide a clear match, and you need more data points, like name, telephone, and address to make the match. Since this is more based on inference, it is called probabilistic matching. Systems have various ways of configuring this automatically. Often a case has to be looked at by a human who can change it. This is called a data steward. The responsibilities of a data steward are to make those decisions about master data and update the source if necessary.

While we have only talked about persons, there are a number of other established data models across industries, like buildings, logistics, and so on. Certain MDM vendors supply these from industry standards or their own best practice. It is also possible to define your own model. The key point is that in order to do master data management, you need to have an authoritative model of the information you want to manage and a decision on where the master of this is.

Data quality

In order to improve the coherence and integrity of the data, there are a number of tools and techniques to improve data quality. These are typically components of data management or MDM software, but data quality can be done without MDM and data governance. Where MDM focuses on actively correcting and making decisions about data, the data quality tools are meant for visualizing and automatically correcting data based on simple rules.

An important part of data quality is data profiling. This is a technique where you can analyze the different attributes of a data entity, to understand if values are mismatched or don't comply with what is expected – for example, if a phone number has letters in it. You can also identify if data is missing. The profiling can also be used for more detailed investigations of whether something looks suspicious, like if one postal code is overrepresented. Data profiling is a purely descriptive process.

The next step in data quality is to automatically correct mistakes. An example would be to insert a default value instead of a missing field. This is part of a process known as data preparation. It could also be to give a warning that the data is not okay and someone has to look at it. Usually data analysts profile the data of a data source before working with it for analysis. This can result in issues reported to the data owner, since he or she is ultimately responsible for the quality of the data.

For an overview of the different aspects of data management see Table 4-4.

Table 4-4. *Data management*

	Organization	Data Level	Responsibility	Process
CDO	Business	Conceptual	Definitions, processes, guidelines	Data governance
Data owner	Business	Logical	Solution ownership, definitions	Data governance
Data steward	Business	Logical	Operational at the data level	MDM
Data analyst	Business/IT	Logical/physical	Operational at the data level, data user	MDM/data quality
Database administrator	IT	Physical	Operational at the physical level	MDM/data quality

Summary

In this chapter, we have taken a deeper look into the different forces that affect how we use data in the city. Understanding the source system is important in order to get to the data and acquiring an understanding of what the data can be used for. Data in source systems can be either structured, semi-structured, or unstructured. This has consequences for how it should be stored and processed. The current market offers many tools for storing data. Each comes with its own set of tradeoffs that need to be taken into account when a solution is built. Some solutions are good for scalability and throughput but not flexible, whereas others are flexible but don't scale well. Having a clear idea about what the data will be used for and typical use cases is key to selecting the right data services. Similarly, the data access pattern has to be determined as there are great differences between having other systems access the data and giving access to human end users.

We saw how there are different options for deploying solutions. This can be done on premise in the organization's own data center or in the cloud. In the cloud, we have different options as well. IaaS is similar to on premise, but a part of the basic responsibilities is taken by the vendor. PaaS sees more of responsibilities taken over by the vendor, while SaaS is similar to buying a prebuilt system. The more responsibility the vendor takes over, the less flexibility the customer has. Making the right decision is based on tradeoffs for a concrete solution.

Increasingly, it is important also to understand the regulatory requirements especially for personal data. This is an area that sees a different focus around the world, but the trend is toward increasing regulation of personal data. While there are differences between areas like health and criminal justice, there are some general measures that need to be taken.

Managing the data is not just a technical endeavor. In order to be successful, many organizations implement a data governance framework that specifies policies, processes, and decision rights. Along with this, support for master data management is usually necessary for complex organizations with data spread out across multiple solutions. Regardless of the level of data governance and master data management, addressing data quality is also a frequent concern.

Understanding and addressing these different forces is crucial for smart city solutions, since cities run on data.

CHAPTER 5

Intelligence

The "Smart" part of smart cities depends crucially on intelligence in the solutions. Cities have used technology for centuries, but what makes a smart city is the use of intelligent solutions. This is where the field of artificial intelligence (AI) comes into play. AI provides some unique opportunities but also a number of challenges. Nevertheless, getting the intelligence right is a key objective for smart cities.

In this chapter, we will learn more about what AI actually is. There is a lot of hype and misconception surrounding this term, so we will provide a solid foundation of the history and technical nature of AI. With this in place, we will look at some key issues for AI in a smart city context. In the end of the chapter, we will look at the differences that affect the use of AI in a smart city context.

The history of AI

The idea of artificial intelligence is not a new one. The thought of infusing intelligence and thinking into inert matter can be traced back to antiquity. In Greek mythology, there are several examples of mechanical contraptions behaving in an intelligent way, like Hephaestus' three-legged tables that moved around his workshop by themselves. Similar stories can be found in Norse, Egyptian, Buddhist, and other mythologies from around the world. It is safe to say that the idea that humans can create intelligent mechanisms is if not universal then at least widespread. In modern times,

© Anders Lisdorf 2020
A. Lisdorf, *Demystifying Smart Cities*, https://doi.org/10.1007/978-1-4842-5377-9_5

intelligent machines have been a mainstay of popular science fiction, and this has driven the thinking about how computers could and should work.

There is no single accepted definition of artificial intelligence, but the Turing test, which is a thought experiment first presented by the British mathematician Alan Turing in 1950, has become an agreed standard criterion for determining artificial intelligence in computers.

The test aims to find out if a machine can exhibit intelligent behavior equivalent to or indistinguishable from a human. The Turing test may be familiar from the 2014 film about him called *The Imitation Game*. The imitation game is actually the central part of the Turing test. It is a game played by three persons: two witnesses of opposite sexes the male (A) and female (B) and an interrogator (C). The interrogator can communicate with A and B only through notes or some other textual medium. The purpose of the game is to determine which witness is which. The male has to try to trick the interrogator. If he succeeds, he wins. The woman wins if she helps the interrogator correctly identify her as the woman and the man as a man. Now, Turing thought, what if the computer substituted the male witness (A) in the game? If the computer is able to, on average, fool the interrogator as often as a human male, it qualifies as artificial intelligence.

Turing preferred the term "Thinking Machines" but was adamant that this had to be a binary computer (although not necessarily electrical). It was not until the summer workshop in 1956 at Dartmouth College that the term artificial intelligence was cemented as the name of the field studying how computers can exhibit humanlike thinking capabilities. Today the list of participants of this workshop reads as a hall of fame in artificial intelligence research.

While conversation is one possible application of AI, it is just one of many tasks for AI in today's world. There are bots that do this kind of test, but the setup is not representative of most types of current AI applications. AI has been generalized to all tasks where a computer can perform indistinguishably from a human. Furthermore, we do not expect AI to be merely indistinguishable from humans; we typically want it to also be superior to humans, whether in precision, scope, time, or some other parameter. We typically want AI to be better than us.

Another thing to keep in mind is a distinction between Artificial General Intelligence (AGI), as measured by the Turing test, and Artificial Narrow Intelligence (ANI), which is an application of humanlike intelligence in a particular area for a particular purpose. In our context, we will not go further into AGI and the philosophical implications of this but focus on ANI since this has many contemporary applications.

The promise and threat of AI

When we think about what AI can do for us, we can think about it in the same way as steam power in the industrial revolution. Steam power made it possible to supplant and improve human power. Rather than having any number of humans or livestock manually performing a task, steam power now would do this instead. The engines were eventually changed to gasoline and electrical power, but the essence is that the industrial revolution boosted human physical power beyond what any single human or group of humans would be capable of.

Similarly, AI promises to boost human mental powers. It promises to perform a number of tasks in a human way with superior performance. Current examples include self-driving cars, diagnostic aids for doctors, recommendations on music and films, and so on. All of these things have been performed by humans, but AI would be able to take them over with superior performance leaving humans to focus on other more interesting or worthwhile tasks. This is similar to the industrial revolution where machines would take over the hard, physical labor making it possible for humans to do something different instead.

Obviously, this is not the only aspect of AI. It also comes with reservations and fear. First of all, it is not clear to everyone that the AI will actually leave jobs for regular humans. It has been suggested, for example, that AI should pay tax in order not to create an unfair advantage for AI on the job market. Another aspect is privacy and transparency. Will AI undermine our democratic and human rights? Will it be fair when it makes decisions? Great concern has been voiced around this already, due to examples of AI showing racial and other biases. Initiatives to secure transparency of algorithms and privacy in AI solutions have taken shape around the world. The ultimate fear is a complete takeover by the machines. This is another central theme of the science fiction genre familiar from *Terminator, 2001, The Matrix*, and so on.

The key challenge for us is to balance the promises with the threats. This means that every solution has to be vetted. We have to be able to curb the techno-optimists, but also to counter the alarmists. I am not sure the right balance has been found yet, but it is something we will have to continuously pursue in multiple fora with a diversity of stakeholders – not just the tech-savvy establishment. Just getting others to join the conversation is a challenge that weighs on the tech industry as much as civic leaders.

What is Artificial Intelligence really?

The basic premise is that intelligence is something humans can recreate and that we can imbue other entities with this intelligence. There are a number of more or less well-defined subfields of artificial intelligence that are sometimes used interchangeably with the term such as machine learning, deep learning, data mining, neural networks, and so on. In practical terms, they all build applications with computer code that implements particular algorithms.

An algorithm is a set of instructions or rules that will provide the solution to a problem. Clearly, not all algorithms are AI. A recipe qualifies as an algorithm but hardly as an intelligent one. It would be fair to say that an AI algorithm would qualify as such if the input given produces a similar output to that of a human being. Take for example the recommendation algorithm familiar from Netflix and Spotify. This is similar to going to the video store or record store and telling the sales person what you like. She would then be able to recommend similar titles based on her knowledge of music or films.

In the field of AI, there are different classes of algorithms for different types of problems. They range from very simple and transparent ones to very complex and opaque ones. People familiar with statistics will know linear regression. This also qualifies as a type of artificial intelligence, because it produces an intelligent guess on something based on input to an algorithm. In the following when we talk about AI here, it is in the sense of machine learning because it is more precise. Machine learning only deals with how computers can perform tasks similar to humans, which is what is relevant in a smart city context.

Machine learning

There are different ways to think about the different types of machine learning, but consensus is that there are three general categories of machine learning algorithms: supervised, unsupervised, and reinforcement learning.

Supervised learning

Supervised learning always requires that the algorithm be given data in the form of examples that it can learn from and extract a pattern that can be used for inference in new situations. This is called training data. From this data, the machine learning algorithm extracts patterns that it can use to identify similar observations based on new data. A typical example is a neural network used to recognize objects. A set of training data has been labeled by humans with the different categories of objects, like chair, door, orange, and cup. The algorithm then processes all the images showing the different instances of these objects. Based on these inputs, it extracts patterns that allow it to detect the different categories in the training set.

The key here is that the algorithm can do this iteratively and get more and more precise. The pattern itself in this case is a black box, but it can be used to detect the objects in new and unknown photos.

Unsupervised learning

Unsupervised learning algorithms do not depend on examples and try to make sense of the data it is given by classifying it. It aims to identify previously unknown patterns in the data. The typical process is to perform clustering. In this case, the algorithm discovers clusters of observations based on how close the observations are. Imagine a scenario where we want to classify people according to their physical characteristics. In the simplest case, we have two dimensions: height and weight. Clusters will maybe form around short and heavy people, tall and heavy people, and so on. You can add another dimension: gender. Still you can identify clusters, but they start to become more distinct. Three dimensions can still be depicted in space. If we add further dimensions, we cannot picture it graphically or mentally anymore, but mathematically it makes no difference. We could add age, annual income, and so on. Based on these parameters, our clusters start to become interesting, because we can classify new cases. We can identify new patterns of people's physical characteristics such as tall middle-aged women from the middle class, which may seem to be a distinct category. There are different techniques for determining what qualifies as a cluster and how strong it is. But the important part is that we can learn new things about the data and discover unknown patterns.

Reinforcement learning

Reinforcement learning differs in that it continually changes and adapts to the problem. Whereas supervised learning builds on a training set and comes up with a model that does not change until next time it is trained, reinforcement learning continues to adapt to the problem based on success or failure. In this way, it works on a balance between exploration (based on discovering new information) and exploitation (using existing information). Still the algorithm needs to know whether it was successful or not; it needs a reward mechanism. The algorithm creates a best guess at what would solve the problem and then it receives feedback on how well it solved it. Going through multiple iterations and new configurations, it gets closer to an optimal solution. This is similar to how a child learns to speak. At first it is babbling. As the child learns, sounds that come close to real words start to appear, and it is rewarded by its parents understanding every time it gets closer to the real pronunciation. This means that it is necessary to set up a function to evaluate the success of an output. These types of algorithm are typically used in types of problems where the parameters interact dynamically with each other as is the case in physics or biology. A simple example from biology would be strength and speed of a given animal. If it grows bigger, it would be better able to defend itself, but it would be harder to escape and catch prey. If it were faster, it could escape and catch prey but may not be strong enough to retain it. Add to this the ecosystem dynamics of predator/prey relationships, and you have a fairly complex function to discover. In this example where we simulate the success of a species, the population size would be the value we could use to optimize.

Popular AI algorithms

There is no one general artificial intelligence algorithm but rather multiple different types tailored to a particular type of problem. There is some overlap between some of them, but in general particular types are used for specific classes of problems. In the following are some of the most commonly used with possible applications for smart cities. Understanding the type of algorithm gives you an indication of the principles of how it works; the details of implementation and optimization are an art form in itself that we will not go further into here.

Linear regression – Perhaps the most basic type of supervised learning is the linear regression known by most people who have taken a basic statistics course. The purpose of linear regression is to predict the dependent variable on the basis of one or more independent variables. An example is unemployment rate. This would be the dependent variable. We would try to predict it using other independent variables like income tax rate, interest rates, wages, and rental costs. The trick here is that if you can find a model where the independent variables have a high degree of influence on the dependent variable, you can start simulating what would happen if you change some of these variables. At a macrolevel, this is a useful tool to guide policy makers and strategy development, but it is also a crude measure that does not adequately take into consideration interaction between variables. It is often used for macrolevel phenomena where you have one clear dependent numerical variable and a number of numerical independent variables. It could therefore be any macro problem where reliable numeric data is available like economic models and tax incentives, traffic flow, or retention of employees.

Logistic regression – The difference between logistic and linear regression is that the logistic regression tries to predict a binary dependent variable. This means that the logistic regression tries to predict, based on a number of independent variables, whether something will happen or not. This could be used in relation to disease or morbidity. Based on a number of independent variables like socioeconomic status, age, and BMI, the logistic regression can predict the probability of death (1) or survival (0). Similar to linear regression, this is a crude measure that does not take into consideration interaction between variables. It would perhaps be useful to inform policy by understanding dropout rates from schools, improving mortality rate based on understanding of factors, or minimizing recidivism by having a more accurate understanding of which criminals should receive special attention.

Support vector machines (SVMs) – It is a learning algorithm that tries to classify observations into one of two classes, like true or false, such that any new data point can be accurately predicted to belong to either of them. The reason it is called a vector is that the input is broken down into any number of inputs in an n-dimensional space. You may recall from your high school math lessons that a vector is an expression of forces in different directions in an n-dimensional space. Each new value along a dimension adds to the vector. Based on the input vector, the SVM is able to determine which class it belongs to. A dimension can be anything that can be expressed numerically. If we think about an example of whether a web shop customer will make a purchase, the relevant dimensions could be previous amount spent, time on site, time of day, and so on. It is mathematically perhaps a bit less transparent than linear regression, but it has definite niches of application. Since it is used for binary classification, it can only be used for yes/no types of problems. It has been used in biology, for detecting handwriting, classification of images, and face detection. It could perhaps be used to detect identity fraud if data exists on a person's handwriting or other writing so as to determine if a piece of text was or was not made by the person.

K-nearest neighbors – Similar to support vector machines, the K-nearest neighbors is a classification algorithm that works in a multidimensional space. Remember that a dimension can be anything. In our retail example, the K-nearest neighbors algorithm could be used to construct customer segments that are similar along the identified dimensions of interest. The K is a number that expresses how many classes should be identified. If you choose K=5, you will end up with five customer segments. Each individual data point, that is, a customer, will belong to one of these classes. This can be used in advertising, discounts, and so on. It may be familiar from Netflix where they identify genres like "Romantic Action Comedies." A cluster of films are found to be similar along a number of dimensions that are fed into the algorithm. Subsequently, you can give them a name by looking at the observations in the cluster. In retail segments could be family with small kids, singles, or pensioners. Because their shopping habits are similar, they form a cluster that can be categorized. This type of algorithm is powerful to identify unknown clusters of observations that are not apparent. In a city context, it could be used to identify people with special needs or habits that are underserved. It could also be to understand different segments' use of public transportation in order to optimize the offering.

Decision trees – Decision trees are simple and transparent to understand. They can however be very powerful. They are used to predict a categorical outcome based on input variables. They can handle both numerical and categorical data as input. The tree is constructed from a root that contains all observations in the training set. At each node, the training set is split according to a variable that is typically categorical like male/female, yellow/green/blue/red, or similar. These categories split the branches of the tree. At the end are the leaves that are the outcome of the decision tree. Let us consider shoppers in a web shop. Let us say we want to classify them according to different tiers like silver, gold, and platinum based on how much they spend per year. The first branch may be age. We split this into <20, 21–50, and >50. Next branch we consider gender. This gives us a powerful instrument to categorize a new customer just based on demographic input. There are certain problems that lend themselves to this like classifying people or observations. On a city web site, this could be used to classify residents in order to route them to appropriate services.

Neural networks – Perhaps the most well-known algorithm associated with artificial intelligence is the neural network. As the name indicates, it is loosely based on how neurons process information. A neuron is characterized by having a lot of connections to other neurons. At one side are the input neurons from which signals are received. At the other side are output neurons that signals are transmitted to. A neuron, based on its input, either activates or not. The threshold is the value beyond which it is activated.

The value of the threshold is essentially what is set in a neural network. It is called a weight. The system learns by a mechanism called backpropagation that adapts the values of the weights based on the success of the system. If the output does not match the expected, the weights are open to change, but the more they are successful, the more fixed the weights become. In the end the system consisting of multiple layers of "neurons" adapts such that the input is transformed to elicit the correct output. This is also what is behind the term deep learning where the number of layers is increased. Contrast this to the decision tree where each layer of the tree gives you a good and comprehensible information about how decisions are made in terms of classification. In a neural net, all you have are layers consisting of weights and connections. This is why it is considered a black box. We have no idea how the neural net splits up the information into discrete patterns and really no way of knowing. We can only stand by and watch the output and decide whether it is accurate. It is great for situations where a lot of information has to be condensed into categorical knowledge like computer vision, where we are interested in parsing an image and extracting data about objects in the image. Use cases for cities would be in computer vision where images could be converted into counts of pedestrians, cars, and bicycles or for allowing speech interaction with city services. The resident could speak, and the input converted into text that could then be processed as questions and answers.

Naïve Bayes – Based on Bayes' theorem, the naïve Bayes algorithm aims to make probabilistic classification based on prior knowledge. Thomas Bayes was an Eighteenth-century English minister and philosopher who first proposed to use conditional probability. The basic assumption is that we can use prior knowledge to determine probabilities. If we know that smoking is an important factor in the probability of developing respiratory illnesses, it can be used to give us a probability of a given person developing a respiratory illness based on his or her smoking habits. Bayesian learning is a family of algorithms that are used in similar circumstances as the logistical regression or other categorical models to predict whether a given observation will belong to one or other of a number of classes. It has, for example, been used for classifying spam messages. Based on a number of parameters, it is possible to assess the probability that a given message is spam. In a city context, it could be used to tailor city services to residents. Let us say that we know a lot about individuals that typically need social services based on their income, number of children, employment history, and so on. This could be used to determine the probability that any given resident will be needing social services.

Genetic algorithms – Inspired by biology, genetic algorithms aim to optimize a solution. This is done by starting from a population of candidate solutions. A solution is a value that would be an optimal solution to the problem at hand. The representation of the solution can vary, but a typical representation is a string of characters. These candidate solutions are evaluated against a fitness function that determines how well they perform. The most successful candidate solutions are then used to create a second generation of candidate solutions by a process of recombination or mutation. These will share many of the traits of the previous most successful generation. Similar to the first generation, they are again evaluated against a fitness function, and the most successful ones are selected as parents for the next generation. This has the possibility to produce optimal solutions in situations where it is not feasible to test for all possible permutations or combinations of traits. It has all the same drawbacks as biological evolution too, such as the problem of local optimum. Imagine you have a fitness curve where you find a bump at some point. The algorithm will try to get closer to this bump even if further along the curve there is a much higher optimum. This is similar to species that evolve to be successful in local areas. It has been used for molecular structure optimization in the pharmaceutical industry and scheduling applications such as NASA's Deep Space Network. For cities it could perhaps be used for optimization of resource utilization like water and energy, because these are not straightforward and have many interacting variables. Another complex optimization problem in cities is traffic flow, where, for example, simulations could be done on the mobility mix between public transportation at different times of the day and year.

For an overview of the advantages and limitations of different types of AI algorithms see Table 5-1.

Table 5-1. *Advantages and limitations of common AI algorithms*

Algorithm Type	Advantages	Limitations
Linear regression	Easy to understand Low computational demand	Only works with numerical variables Does not capture interaction between variables
Logistical regression	Easy to understand Low computational demand	Only predicts a binary outcome Does not capture interaction between variables
Support vector machines	Works with unstructured information	Categorizes only into two categories that need to be defined Significant computational demand
K-nearest neighbors	Identifies new clusters that are not apparent Classifies observations into multiple categories	Clusters need to be interpreted as they don't make sense by themselves
Decision trees	Transparent Powerful to understand and predict behavior	Simplistic Limited to problems that have a tree-like structure Works best with categorical input

(continued)

Table 5-1. (*continued*)

Algorithm Type	Advantages	Limitations
Neural networks	Processes any type of information Can mimic human classification	Not transparent how it works Needs pre-classification by humans Significant computational demand
Naïve Bayes	Using existing knowledge to predict probabilities of occurrence	Needs data about prior occurrences
Genetic algorithms	Finds the optimal solution in a problem space Captures interaction between variables	There has to be a well-defined utility function for the problem Significant computational demand

Key issues in AI for Smart Cities

Using artificial intelligence in a city context raises a lot of questions that Turing's initial thought experiment never addressed. Humans expect much more and much different than just having a conversation with something behaving in a human way when it impacts their daily lives. In many cases, they expect superhuman capabilities and, in others, not so much. It's complicated. This complication is important to understand in order for artificial intelligence to be successful in smart city contexts and not to develop into a new veiled technocracy or be rejected outright by the masses. We need to focus on how AI will work in the real world. First, we will look at some examples of how the real world poses challenges to AI solutions, and then we will focus on understanding the different forces affecting AI solutions for smart city applications.

Artificial and human intelligence

Artificial intelligence has made impressive progress in the last couple of decades. Some of the more iconic ones that made the headlines around the world are the following:

- IBM's Deep Blue beats Russian Chess Grandmaster Garry Kasparov (1990s).

- IBM's Watson beats world champions Ken Jennings and Brad Rutter in *Jeopardy* (2000s).

- Google's AI beats world champion in Go Lee Se-dol (2010s).

What more could we want to show us that it is just a matter of time before AI becomes truly human in its ability? The average observer would be forgiven for thinking that truly intelligent machines are right around the corner. But while these problems are hard for humans and indeed show immense human skills, they are comparatively easy for artificial intelligence. None of these are really hard problems for an AI. This has to do with how AI works.

Notice that one thing is common for all three examples: the goals are very clear. Chess, *Jeopardy*, and Go: you either win or you don't. This is similar to other successful AI applications like facial and speech recognition: you either recognize the person or you don't. As we saw previously, AI is good at finding solutions to types of problems where you have a very well-defined correct solution. If only human life were so simple. Virtually all of human life does not have a well-defined right or wrong. This is why management and self-help literature is filled with advice around how important it is to set goals.

When you were a child, did you know what you wanted to work with? Did you know the precise attributes of your prospective spouse? Did you ever change your mind? Did you ever want to do two or more mutually exclusive things, like eating cake for breakfast and losing weight? Being human we are so used to constantly evaluate tradeoffs, with unclear and frequently changing goals that we don't even think about it. This is not just hard but downright impossible for any current artificial intelligence.

Autonomous vehicles and ethics

Let us look at this through the lens of an existing AI problem. Today many cities have begun allowing companies to test autonomous vehicles (AV) on their streets. On virtually every parameter, they are performing well and well above their human counterparts if the vendors are to be trusted. There is the occasional accident that spurs quite a lot of media attention. Given the low scale AV testing is currently carried out, this will be amplified significantly when it is rolled out. While the autonomous vehicles are very good at following rules and identifying the proper ones in a given situation, what happens in situations where the rules might be conflicting and they even have to make a tradeoff decision with ethical impact?

Here is a thought experiment to illustrate the issue. An autonomous vehicle is driving on a sunny spring afternoon through the streets of New York. It is a good day, and it is able to keep a good pace. On its right is a sidewalk with a lot of pedestrians; on its left is a traffic lane going the opposite direction. Now suddenly a child runs out into the road in front of the AV, and it is impossible for it to brake in time. The autonomous vehicle needs to make a choice. It has three options:

1) It runs over the child and kills it while not hurting the people inside the AV or the pedestrians on the sidewalk.

2) It makes an evasive maneuver to the right hitting pedestrians, thereby killing or injuring one or more people while not hurting the people inside the AV.

3) It makes an evasive maneuver to the left hitting cars going the other direction, thereby killing the people in the AV and the people in the other car but sparing the child and the pedestrians. For a summary of outcomes of the autonomous vehicle disaster see Table 5-2.

Table 5-2. *Autonomous vehicle disaster scenarios*

Scenario	Child	Pedestrians	Opposite Car	AV
1	Dies	Survive	Survive	Survive
2	Survives	Die	Survive	Survive
3	Survives	Survive	Die	Die

How do we prepare the AI to make that decision? Now, the goals are not so clear as in a game of *Jeopardy*. This is not a zero-sum game where you either win or lose. Humans make moral judgments in situations like this and are aided by ethical values. But what are they?

Is it more important not to hurt children at any price? Let's just say for the sake of argument this was the key value. The AI would then have to calculate how many children were on the sidewalk and in a given car on the opposite side of the road. It may kill two children on the sidewalk or in another car. What if there were two children in the autonomous vehicle itself? Does the age factor in to the decision? Is it better to kill old people than younger? The AI would then have to scan people and try to identify their age before it makes a decision, which is technically perfectly feasible. What about medical conditions? Would it not be better to hit a terminal cancer patient than a healthy young mother? The AI would have to try to extract medical information maybe look up medical records based on facial recognition that identified the social security number of the person. This is also perfectly feasible even in real time with today's technology.

As should be clear, this line of reasoning is one that humans prefer not to go into, but that would be necessary since the AI in the autonomous vehicle needs someone to tell it what to do or at least give it a set of values to make it possible to arrive at a decision.

The point of this thought experiment is just to highlight that even if the AI could make an optimal decision, it is not simple what optimal means and there is no way that we could ever reach a consensus. It is incredibly easy to reach consensus on who wins or loses in Chess, *Jeopardy*, and Go, but even the simplest human moral judgments are bound to be contested.

There are hundreds of thousands of similar situations where there just by definition is no one right solution, and consequently no clear goal we can train the AI against. What if we had an AI as the next president? Would we trust it to make the right decisions in all cases? Probably not, politics is about sentiment, subjectivity, and hard solutions. Would we entrust an AI that would be able to go through all previous court cases, statistics, and political objectives to make fair rulings and sentencing? No way, although it probably could.

It seems evident that AI must always be explained in terms of human intelligence. We would still have to instill the heuristics and the tradeoffs in the AI, which then leads back to who programs or trains the AI. Will we then have technology corporations and their programmers making key moral decisions about who lives and dies in our cities? They will be the intelligence inside the artificial intelligence if no one else steps in.

In many ways, this is already the case. A more peaceful case in point is online dating: a programmer has essentially decided who should find love and who shouldn't through the matching algorithm and the input used. Inside the AI is the programmer making decisions no one ever agreed they should. Artificial General Intelligence is as elusive as ever – no matter how many resources we throw at AI and no matter how impressive it can be at simple games. Life will throw us the same problems as it always has, and at the end of the day, the intelligence will be human anyway.

Artificial Intelligence meets the real world

Another important constraint for AI is ecological – not in the sense of the tech ecosystem consisting of different vendors, projects, and organizations. Here I am thinking about the total ecosystem in which AI technology has to exist. In the city, humans have to interact and bear the consequences of the technology that AI powers. This introduces new considerations that are important to keep in mind. First of all, there is the fact that any system in a city will interact with other systems creating system-level complex dynamics that can be difficult to predict. Second is the very basic fact that the people of the city who will reap the benefits or suffer the consequences are voters who keep or change the politicians in power. And ultimately politicians fund AI.

Frequently at conferences or in the media, you will hear about the transformative power of AI on all aspects of city life. But once you dig deeper and look at current deployments, it is difficult to see that this is transformative and not just incremental gains. We have the intelligent trash bins; some cities have surveillance that detects gunshots and stolen cars. There are also impressive results from POCs for intelligent traffic regulation in Atlanta, Pittsburg, and San Diego where travel time has been reduced between 10% and 25% in central corridors. Still less than 1% of traffic lights in the United States are intelligent today. You may wonder why since mobility is usually a top 3 concern of residents in cities and huge amounts of fuel are wasted in idling engines. Is this not a win-win situation?

In order to understand why so little traffic regulation is "smart" when the upside has been demonstrated to be immense, we have to take a more systemic approach. In New York City, there has been known to be congestion, and we want to improve that. Let us say that we are able to construct an AI system like the one from San Diego, Atlanta, or Pittsburg that could optimize traffic flow throughout the city – not just a single or a few selected corridors but the whole city. This will not be a simple or easy task but also not outside the realm of possibilities. Let us say that all traffic lights are connected to this central AI algorithm that provides the city as a whole with optimal traffic conditions. The algorithm works on sensor input that counts the number of cars and their speed at different intersections based on traffic cameras. Let us say that our theoretical system provides the same improvements in travel times as the corridors that have been piloted and the whole city suddenly on average gets 10% faster to and from work. Everyone should be happy.

Now imagine during one of the congestions that still occur although not as often, a fire erupts in downtown Manhattan and fire trucks are delayed in traffic due to this congestion. Fifty people die. The media then finds out that the traffic lights are controlled by an artificial intelligence algorithm. They ask the Commissioner of Transportation why 50 people had to die because of an algorithm. Perhaps it's not fair but a very realistic scenario. She tries to explain that the algorithm optimizes the overall flow of traffic and doesn't make congestion go away altogether. The media are skeptical and ask her to explain how it works. This is where it gets complicated. Since this is a neural network algorithm that functions like a black box, no one can really tell precisely how it works or why there was a congestion delaying the fire trucks at that particular time. The outrage is palpable, and headlines read "City Has Surrendered to Deadly AI," "50 People Die due to Intelligent Traffic System," and "Incomprehensible Algorithm Leads to Incomprehensible Fatalities."

In addition, the system-level properties of such an optimization will also lead to some areas of the city seeing an increase in travel times and others a decrease. Humans are constituted such that they pay attention very selectively. They overrepresent negative experiences. If we merge this with excessive use of social media, this will be hugely amplified, and quickly social media will have trending stories of how traffic is much worse with the new intelligent system than in the old days even though there is a proven 10% increase in travel times.

Contrast this to a simple algorithm that is based on clear and simple rules that are not as effective overall but work along the lines of 30 seconds one way and 30 seconds another way. Who would blame the Commissioner of Transportation for congestion in that case? Who would blame the travel time on the algorithm in the traffic lights? Today this is how it works. These timers are set in advance based on simulations that were done at a specific point in time. Everyone knows the way this works and just considers congestion a fact of life. While travel times may be faster, satisfaction with the system is lower.

Let us say that we were able to curb the dissatisfaction and through first-class public relations, residents would realize that everything is actually better. There could still be other unwanted effects due to system-level dynamics that would not be known in advance. Let us assume that the AI system gets continuous input about traffic flow in the city. Based on this feed, it can adapt the signals to optimize the flow. This is great, but due to the fact that we now have coupled the system with thousands of feedback loops, it enters into the realm of complex or chaotic systems and will start to exhibit properties that are associated with that kind of systems. Typical examples of such properties are erratic behavior, path dependency, and limited possibility for prediction. The system could develop quirks like keeping one light red all the time because it is the most effective for traffic flow as a whole. It could also introduce resonance and ripple effects. Even massively scalable AI cannot counteract these effects easily because they are systemwide properties of which the AI itself is a part.

Even if we could adapt the system, the true system dynamics would not be known until the system goes live. We would not know how many cars would be running red lights or speed up/slow down compared to today. Possibly the system could be trimmed and be made to behave, but then we have to think about political realities. Which responsible leader would want to experiment with a city of more than 8 million peoples' daily lives? Who would want to face these people and explain to them that the reason they are late for work or for their son's graduation is that the city is currently trimming its AI algorithm?

System-level effects are very real and are not predictable from the design of the solution. There are of course ways around this, but it is something entirely different from common IT systems that can be tested and approved in advance because the performance is known to be the same live as in test.

The optimization paradox

We have been considering how to pave the way for AI to make life in a city better, safer, more prosperous, and equitable. We want AI to optimize functions to the benefit of the city, but there are important exceptions in the real world where residents may not appreciate optimizations no matter how much better they will make things.

I believe the following is a familiar feeling to any of my fellow motorists: the letter in the mail displaying your innocent face at the wheels of your car and a registered speed higher than allowed along with payment details of the ticket you received for the violation. It is interesting to observe the anger we feel and the unmistakable sense that this is deeply unfair even though it is obviously not. The fine is often the result of an automated speed camera that doesn't even follow normal working hours or lunch breaks (an initial reason for it being unfair). A wide suite of mobility products like GPS, scanners, and Waze keeps track of these speed cameras in real time. Some people follow and report this with something approaching religious zeal. But what is the problem here? People know or should know the speed limit and know you will get a ticket if you are caught. The operative part of this sentence seems to be the "if you are caught" part. More about that in a minute.

While working with the city of New York, we piloted a system that would use a computer vision AI to detect different things in traffic. It was not funded beyond the hours we could put into it, so we needed to get people excited and find a sponsor to take this solution we were working on further. Different suggestions about what we should focus on came up. One of them was that we should use the system to detect traffic violations and automatically fine car owners based on the license plate. This is completely feasible; I have received tickets myself based on my license plate, so we gathered that the technology would be a minor issue. With our system, we could then roll it out on all the approximately 3000 traffic cameras that are already in the city. Imagine how much revenue that could bring in. It could probably sponsor a couple of new parks or sports grounds. At the same time, it would improve traffic flow because less people would double-park or park in bus lanes and so on. When you look at it, it seems like a clear win-win solution. We could improve traffic for all New Yorkers and build new parks. We felt pretty confident.

This is where things got complicated. We quickly realized that this was indeed not a pitch that would energize anyone, at least not in a way that was beneficial to the project. Even though people are getting tickets today and do not suggest seriously that they should not, the idea of OPTIMIZING this function in the city seemed completely off. This seems to be a general phenomenon in technological solutions. I call this the "Technology Optimization Paradox": when optimizing a function which is deemed good and relevant leads to resistance at a certain optimization threshold. If the function is good and valuable, there should be no logical reason why doing it better should be worse, but this is in some cases how people feel. It is often seen in the area of law enforcement where we know it as the fear of big brother and the surveillance state. We don't want massive surveillance even though that would greatly increase the fight against terrorism, violent crimes, and similar. We want to optimize the ability of law enforcement to arrest suspects and expose terrorist plots, but we don't want to open our phones to pervasive eavesdropping even though that may be the most effective. We don't want to optimize beyond a certain threshold.

This is where we get back to the "If you are caught" part. Everyone agrees that it is fair that you are punished for a crime if you are caught. The emphasis here is on the "if." When we use technology like AI, we get very very close to substituting the "if" with a "when." This is what we feel is unfair. It is as though we have an intuitive expectation that we should have a fair chance of getting away with something, a right to "stochastic liberty": the right for the individual to have events be undeterministic – especially adversary events. We want to have the liberty to have a chance to get away with a transgression. This is the issue many people have with AI when it is used for certain types of tasks, specifically tasks that have an optimization paradox. It takes away the stochastic liberty; it takes away the chance element.

Let us look at some other examples. When we do blood work, do we want AI to automatically tell us about all our hereditary diseases, so the doctor can tell us that we need to eat more fiber and stop smoking? No, sir, we quietly assert our right to stochastic liberty and the idea that maybe we will be among the 1% who lives to be 90 fueled on a diet of sausages, fries, and milkshake even though half our family died of heart attacks before they turned 40. But do we want AI to detect lung cancer if we suspect that we have it? Yes please!

Do we want AI to automatically detect when we have put too many deductions on our tax return? No way, we want our stochastic liberty. Somebody in the tax department must sit sweating and justify why a regular citizen's tax returns are being looked through. At most we can accept the occasional spot test (like the rare traffic police officer, who also has to take a break and get lunch and check the latest sport results, that's fair). But do we want AI to help us find systematic money laundering and tax evasion schemes? Yes please!

This is a lesson you don't have to explain to politicians who ultimately run the city and decide what gets funded and what not. They know that unhappy people getting too many traffic tickets that they think are unfair will not vote for them. This is a point that often escapes AI proponents when they talk about how we can use AI to make the city a better place. The city is a real place where technology makes real impact on real people and the dynamics of technology solutions exceed those of the system in isolation. Human nature has many quirks that are difficult to understand and explain, and they have nothing to do with the efficiency of the solution.

The challenges to AI

As can be gathered from the preceding examples, the challenges to AI adoption in smart cities may not be primarily of a technical nature. They may have just as much to do with how the people and the world respond. Even if it is better to reduce travel times by 10%, it will still happen that 50 people lose their lives in a fire in Manhattan and some people will have longer travel times to get to work. The stories written will be about the one tragic event and the few negative experiences of residents not about the generally improved trend. Voters remember the headlines and will never notice a smaller trend no matter how positive. Consequently, regardless of the technical utility and precision of AI, there will be cases where the ecology of AI will constrain the solutions more than any code, technology, or infrastructure.

Based on these thought experiments, the most important challenges to adoption of AI solutions at city scale are the following:

> **Unclear benefits** – What are the benefits of leveraging AI for smart cities? We can surely think up a few use cases, but it is harder than you think. Traffic was one but even here the benefits can be elusive. There needs to be a vision and a compelling transformative agenda to drive AI adoption to the next level. Currently we see mainly isolated, siloed, and incremental improvements, and residents need to be given a clear understanding of what the

benefits are for them in order for AI not to be just a fad that the techno elite is pushing while they pat each other on the back at conferences.

Public demand for transparency – If we are ready to let our lives be dominated by AI in any important area, citizens who vote will want to understand precisely how the algorithms work. A fundamental principle of liberal democracies, which many cities have, is transparency in the legal and public administration. The technical nature of much of AI does not align well with that assumption. As we saw previously, many classes of AI algorithms are incomprehensible in their nature and constantly changing. How can we know why it reached that conclusion and how can I examine whether the assumptions were wrong and challenge it? Real people who are late for work or are denied bail will want to know why, and sometimes the Department of Investigation will want to know as well. New York City passed the Local Law 49 in 2018 as the first in the United States in order to require algorithmic transparency in all city systems. The EU's General Data Protection Regulation also aims to provide transparency in how personal data is used and processed.

Political accountability – Whatever an algorithm is doing, people will want to hold a person accountable for it if something goes wrong. Humans have a natural inclination to look for intentional actors, and a machine does not qualify as such. We will want a proper human to be responsible. Who is accountable for malfunctioning AI? Or even proper functioning AI with unintended consequences? We can go through complicated court cases and point the finger at the vendor or the agency sourcing the system, but in a city context, the buck stops with the responsible at the top, the elected or appointed official.

Unacceptable implementation risk – Real-world AI in a city context can rarely be adequately tested in advance as we are used to for other enterprise applications. Implementing and adapting a real-world system may have too many adversarial effects before it starts to be beneficial. No matter how much we prepare, we can never know exactly how the system will behave at scale until we release it in the wild. For a class of systems that are critical for a city, this risk is unacceptable.

The unpredictable human element – With technology in general, it is always unpredictable how people will respond to the solution. Think back on the Google Glass story where Google was completely taken off guard that people could think anything negative about their new and innovative gadget. With artificial intelligence, this unpredictability is exacerbated since the technological solution now has human qualities to it. Some will start relating to it and expecting human and superhuman performance; others will feel uneasy. As we have seen already with autonomous vehicles, it is sure to draw headlines and create its own dynamics.

Artificial intelligence is a great technological opportunity for cities, but we have to develop approaches for how to mitigate the negative effects of AI in order to arrive something that is truly beneficial at scale.

AI solutions in the city

As we saw previously, there are a number of challenges to AI. These can be thought of as a number of forces that operate on the use of AI in a city context. The discussion in tech media seems to revolve only around one of these, that is, the technical possibilities. If we look at Figure 5-1, we can see that this is only one part of the picture.

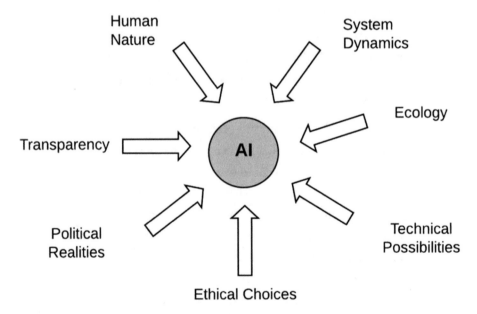

Figure 5-1. *Forces affecting AI solutions in the city*

Human nature – As we saw previously, human nature has its quirks that are difficult but no less important to understand in order to be successful in implementing AI solutions. The field of behavioral economics is dedicated to studying the different biases that guide how we humans form opinions and make decisions. This should be an integral part of any deployment of an AI system, which is something completely new to technology solution development. This has traditionally just been one where a requirement specification guides development. The requirement specification process is traditionally focused on eliciting system requirements from the business side. A selection of people with domain knowledge document what is needed. The problem here is that even people with domain knowledge will not necessarily be experts in human nature and another set of experts may be needed.

Transparency – While technology has always been somewhat of a black box for its users and those who commission it, AI only exacerbates this state of affairs. In more traditional IT development, it has been customary to document algorithms in pseudo code or even words, and the performance could be checked by users knowing these algorithms. With many types of AI, this transparency has disappeared. First of all, even if we could understand the algorithm, it is not clear how this is implemented. Second, the performance of the algorithm may be continuously changing or depend on the training data that someone decided to feed it. A training set can consist of hundreds of thousands or millions of observations. In order to understand the performance of the algorithm, one would have to go through this. Recently a movement is picking up around the world to ensure transparency in city technology.

Political realities – The political realities are not a black box but more of a dark horse. It is unpredictable and does not follow the laws of traditional logic. The media, trends, and fads may intervene at any point, which can be an advantage or disadvantage but definitely something that needs to be tracked. Most people in city administration have a pretty good feeling about the political agenda and how that will impact the success for the AI project. This of course can change with changing administrations, so it is a definite risk for any high-profile project.

Ethical choices – The ethical dimension is one that is coming into focus as AI solutions are approaching prime-time exposure. People start asking questions about decisions and consequences from AI solutions, most notably the advent of autonomous vehicles. These solutions present us with a unique challenge because artificially intelligent systems are expected to perform in a humanlike capability and consequently expected to make moral judgments on the fly. This means that some sort of ethical guideline has to be implemented. Many high-profile failures of AI systems come from the fact that they didn't take this into consideration. They may develop racist or other inappropriate response patterns because that is what the data tells them. Consequently, an ethical review of AI solutions is in place. We must reflect on the ethics that are built into the system, and it must be transparent who made that decision.

Technical possibilities – The technical possibilities are advancing as we speak, and things that were incredibly hard and would take months of development and substantial computing power when I started working with AI a decade ago are now point and click services that anyone can implement. The tech giants seem to be outdoing each other by the minute with ever more impressive achievements. This will provide an ever-increasing stream of possibilities that can inspire new solutions that can improve virtually any aspect of city life. Even with this state of affairs, it still takes some knowledge of how AI works in order to leverage these possibilities. Consequently, education and training become important to adapt existing resources to the new world of smart cities powered by AI.

Ecology – The city as an ecosystem is also an important consideration when working with AI solutions. A city consists of many different subsystems, and any intervention is bound to create an effect on the ecosystem. This can be hard to understand in detail in advance of a system implementation, but effort should be put into understanding this aspect. For example, if suddenly all busses become autonomous, a lot of bus drivers become unemployed, and how does this affect the city? In general, the prospect of AI is envisioned to have a substantial impact on the labor market which will ripple through society. There is not yet a consensus about whether the net effect will be good or bad, but it is certain to change the ecology of the city. With every smart city solution, attention should also be given to how this will impact other aspects of city life rather than just focusing narrowly on the solution at hand since ultimately in a city context it may affect the success of the solution if the net effect for the city is negative.

System dynamics – Complex systems are notoriously difficult to handle, which can be seen from disasters like the Challenger explosion, Chernobyl and Fukushima, and so on. City technology has not traditionally been complex systems. Rather they have been of a linear and continuous nature. Complex systems are defined by a high number of possible system configurations and often also multiple interacting feedback mechanisms, which produces puzzling and nonlinear effects. Still, few AI implementations have approached the complexity of a true complex system, but they will eventually when they scale. This poses novel challenges for city technologists who are not used to dealing with complex systems, and this will impact everything related to how the system is managed and maintained. Traditional monitoring and support processes that are linear have to be challenged. Scaling AI will require expertise from industries that are used to developing, maintaining, and managing complex systems.

Making cities smarter with AI

Attention toward all these forces that shape the ultimate success of an AI solution is necessary for our cities to become smarter. Today this is happening much in the way of the pack donkey that we saw in Chapter 1 in ad hoc steps that always find the easiest way forward. This leads to a quirky city difficult to manage like the medieval city. Perhaps it is time to try the way of man with its structured approach that would entail addressing all the different forces identified previously in a principled way. There are already examples of such initiatives for some of them.

Solution spotlights

Project Alvelor

New York like many cities has thousands of traffic cameras that are not used for anything besides looking at traffic. Nevertheless, important information about traffic patterns could be gained from these cameras that would be interesting for the city's residents. In order to explore this, the city engaged with its residents to work on a solution that would be open source. The cooperation resulted in a POC that used a computer vision algorithm to categorize and count what it saw. In this way, the first ever data set that over the course of months could tell how many cars, trucks, and busses were on the roads was created. This gave the first picture of the pulse of the city, when traffic is peaking, and what the ratio between trucks, busses, and cars is at different times of day. This is an example of how city and civic groups can work together to develop solutions – in this case, an AI solution that was open sourced for other cities to use and build on.

Amsterdam 311

One foundational problem for residents in any city is to get through to those responsible to solve their problems. There is an anecdote that Mayor Bloomberg once saw a fire hydrant leaking. He asked who was responsible. First, they thought police, then fire department. It ended up being the Department of Environmental Protection. But the important insight was that if the mayor could not even find those responsible, then how could residents? This is how the iconic 311 service was created. It has now been copied by multiple cities in the United States and around the world. The concept is that residents can call with whatever problem they have and 311 will route it to the proper agency. This requires a lot of people taking the phone at all hours of the day. Later came self-service to receive the initial request, but how does a resident know how to categorize a problem according to city organization in order to route it to the proper agency? We are back to the initial problem Bloomberg faced.

In Amsterdam they implemented a system similar to 311. They solved this challenge by using AI to categorize what the request pertains to. Currently it can distinguish 60+ categories. It has handled 300,000 requests. Before this system was implemented, 25% was classified as other. Classification errors are also minimized. With this system, service is more quickly routed with the use of less resources resulting in better service using less resources.

Summary

In this chapter, we have considered the history of AI and the main classes of supervised, unsupervised, and reinforcement learning. There are different algorithms in each different class that carries their own strengths and weaknesses. Choosing the right one for the use case is crucial for success.

However, understanding the techniques is just a small part of the puzzle. Once AI hits reality, a whole new realm of issues arises from expectations and human nature. These are not logical or technical but are very real issues for people living in cities. Examples include who decides the ethical choices of an AI, how precise an AI should be, and a slew of political and practical challenges.

In order to find a way for AI to deliver on its potential, it is necessary to understand the many forces that affect AI in a smart city context: of which just one, technical possibilities, is the main focus today. Equal attention must be paid to human nature, system dynamics, ecology, ethical choices, political realities, and transparency. A holistic focus on these aspects is necessary for AI to realize its potential for cities.

CHAPTER 6

Engagement

In order to build any smart city solution, the city has to engage with stakeholders supplying technology and expertise. This could be a minimal engagement where the city builds everything itself and only technology is sourced from vendors to a maximal solution where the city engages with a contractor to build a turnkey solution. But before we get that far, we have to pause and think about what the city wants to build and whether it fits their profile. Any innovative solution comes with a potential payoff, but it also comes with an associated risk. This goes for technologies as well as engagement models. We need to reflect on the potentials and risks and match this with the city context and match them with the right engagement models.

Technology adoption curve

You may be familiar with terms such as bleeding edge and legacy technology. Both of these terms hint at the fact that technologies have a life cycle they go through. Technologies which we call legacy today, like the wired telephones, are now rarely used, but were considered bleeding edge when they first came out. In the beginning very few were using it, and today very few are using it, but the difference between the few that use legacy technologies and bleeding edge technology could not be greater. As the adoption of the phone shows, there was a time where it hit mass market and virtually everyone used a telephone.

© Anders Lisdorf 2020
A. Lisdorf, *Demystifying Smart Cities*, https://doi.org/10.1007/978-1-4842-5377-9_6

All technological innovations go through this life cycle with a stunning regularity. This was initially discovered by Everett Rogers and published in his seminal book *Diffusion of Innovations* from 1962. The key insight was that technological innovations diffused according to a normal distribution (see Figure 6-1).

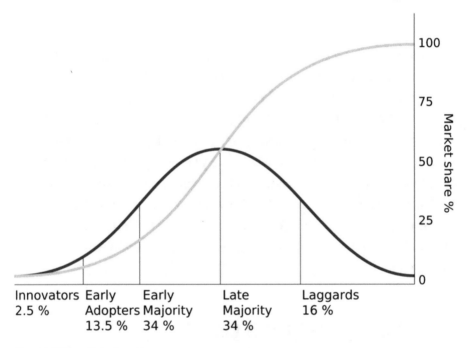

Innovators Early   Early   Late   Laggards
2.5 %   Adopters Majority   Majority   16 %
           13.5 %   34 %   34 %

Source: Wikimedia commons

Figure 6-1. *The diffusion of innovation curve*

This is what explains why only few use the bleeding edge and legacy technologies and most are in the middle. According to Rogers, five distinct adopter categories could be distinguished:

- **Innovators** – Will adopt almost anything as long as it has potential. This group uses the bleeding edge technologies that are experimental and unproven. It also has a high-risk tolerance.

- **Early adopters** – Are more selective than the innovators but put high emphasis in being first. They often look for a first-mover advantage in terms of adopting technology.

- **Early majority** – This group is open to innovation but likes to see it demonstrated by others first. This is one of the largest groups.

- **Late majority** – Adopt innovation after half of the market has already adopted it. They are skeptical and are also often driven by very low-risk tolerance in terms of technology.

- **Laggards** – Are the ones buying legacy technologies when most others have gotten rid of them. They have an aversion to change. This is also a small group.

While the model was initially developed with a focus on individuals, it applies equally well to organizations. When you walk into any IT department, you can immediately recognize the group based on the technologies they use. Similarly, certain cities seem to drive innovation and are open to everything new. These are the ones you hear mentioned frequently at smart city conferences like London, San Jose, Seoul, Barcelona, Singapore, Rio de Janeiro, Amsterdam, and Copenhagen. Others are holding back, while most are somewhere in between.

The reason this is important is that smart city technologies similarly fall on this adoption curve. It is therefore important to understand where on the adoption curve a technology is before deciding to adopt it. Imagine trying to sell a smart watch to someone who just bought a new cabled telephone. Surely that person would not gain the optimal value from this watch. Similarly, imagine selling a fax machine to someone who just bought the latest smartphone after spending the night in line in front of the store. This person would likewise not get much value from the technology.

However, many technologies don't even make it to the mass market and disappear if the early adopters do not catch on to it.

Risk and Reward

Technology adoption is tied to risks and rewards. We do not use technology unless there is some sort of reward, but any new technology is also associated with a risk. The reward is some form of utility. It could be monetary such as cost savings or increased earnings. For a city, it will frequently be something else such as convenience, sustainability, safety, ecological impact, or any other parameter that addresses people's lives or political agendas. This makes it harder to quantify but no less real. Some risks are project specific, while others are generic such as the risk of delay, the risk that solution doesn't work, or that it simply will not be used by people.

Different quadrants will have to be approached differently and depend on the city's strategy (see Figure 6-2).

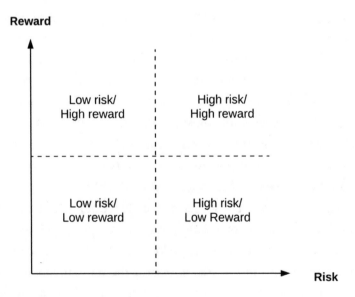

Figure 6-2. *Risk-reward diagram*

If we look at Figure 6-2, we can see four quadrants emerge:

1. **Low risk/low reward** - A lot of work falls in this quadrant. Some of it is work that has to be done; other consists of optimizations that are incremental in nature. These projects are rarely controversial, and everyone will have some amount of these.

2. **Low risk/high reward** - These are the most attractive projects to identify, and decision makers will want to maximize investment here. These projects cater to the first half of the innovation curve, since they often involve the use of new technology.

3. **High risk/low reward** - At the face of it, no one would want to voluntarily fund these projects. However, many projects fall here. Examples are infrastructure maintenance or projects done because of regulatory or legal requirements. The last half of the innovation curve often find themselves doing many projects here.

4. **High risk/high reward** - Some call these moonshots. This type of project typically has a transformative potential for some aspects. It is mostly innovators and early majority that engage in these. Late majority and laggards would never engage in this.

Types of work

Implementing and managing a smart city requires different types of work that all have different risk/reward profiles. All of them are needed and done on a daily basis. Some of the most common are the following:

Business as usual – These are implementations that are done routinely by the organization. If they develop software, this is just a new module or feature made on well-known infrastructure and well-known technologies. Everyone will know more or less what they have to do.

Maintenance – This work is something that needs to be done in order for existing solutions and services not to degrade. This means that ideally there will be no changes in functionality, but other system qualities like resilience, availability, security, and so on are maximized. Examples include upgrades and patching.

Modernization – Sometimes a solution or parts of it become unfeasible to maintain, for example, due to the technology going out of support or no one knows how it works any more. In this case, refactoring a solution or moving it to another technology platform is necessary. Here the technology is new, but the functional properties will remain more or less the same.

Net New – Developing new functionality either from the bottom or using prebuilt components is a standard task that most organizations do to some extent. These span the spectrum from small new systems to major implementations. In most technology organizations, the bulk of work is being done here.

Experimental – These projects are exploratory in nature and are done mainly to learn. This is a traditional R&D, where the upside is very high and the risk similarly high. This type of work often precedes or forms the basis of Net New projects.

If we plot these types of work on a graph, we can see how they cover different quadrants of the risk/reward matrix (see Figure 6-3).

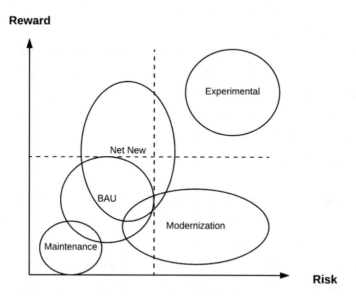

Figure 6-3. Types of work and risk/reward profile

Modes of working

There are a number of different ways to do the types of work we have identified. Some are better for some types of work than others.

Demo – A demo is a generic showcase of out-of-the-box functionality of a solution. It can be done with data similar to the target area. The demo is a good way to ascertain potential solutions before committing to try them out. A demo is small, and many can be carried out. These are used for more experimental types of work.

Proof of concept – A POC is a tailored adaptation of a system solution to a well-defined problem area. It can work with test data, but it has to be as close as possible to the target area. Proofs of concepts are done in order to make sure that an identified solution will work. It requires some more planning and project management to do so; at most a few candidate solutions are POC'ed. POCs are mostly used for experimental and Net New development. It is also sometimes used for particularly risky modernizations.

Pilot – A pilot is a working solution with real production data being used by the intended real-world audience. A pilot almost requires the same as a full implementation project and is often used as a way of making a phased release of a new solution. It is only used for Net New development. The caveat with pilots is that they end up being in production even though they may not have been fully built out to scale to production.

Waterfall – A traditional waterfall project is one that has well-defined deliverables and budget in advance of its commencement and aims to deliver a new solution in production. The traditional waterfall project methodologies are PRINCE2, PMI, and others. They can be used for any type of work no matter how big or small. It is often used for Net New implementations. The waterfall is a bit more prevalent in the public sector because its reliance on predefined deliverables and budgets lends itself well to the prevailing mode of procurement. It has come into disfavor in the technology world due to its high overhead and emphasis on planning ahead of implementation. This is also the reason it does not align well with more unpredictable and smaller implementations that are more exploratory.

Iterative – An iterative project has a dedicated project team and a process for flexibly delivering solution elements, fixes, and augmentations. There are also different frameworks for iterative development like Scrum and SAFe, but a traditional team working in a line of business on a solution area also typically works iteratively. It has been used for decades for business as usual and later with agile development as an emerging standard for Net New development too. With continuous integration/continuous delivery, it has entered the realm of maintenance and infrastructure development. It is also well suited for experimental work since it is good at adapting to new situations. Iterative development is often challenged in its ability to make long-term plans and achieve strategic results since everything is done in small incremental loops. This is why it doesn't lend itself to complex modernizations and certain types of Net New development.

Table 6-1. *Modes of working suitability for different types of work*

	Demo	POC	Pilot	Waterfall	Iterative
BAU				+	+++
Maintenance				+	+++
Modernization		+		+++	+
Net New	++	++	++	+++	++
Experimental	+	++		+	++

Consider Table 6-1 where the different modes of work are shown in columns against the different types of work in rows. A plus in a cell indicates that a given mode of work can be used for a given type of work. Two plusses that it works well for this type of work and three that it is the preferred mode of working for a given type of work. The more plusses, the more efficient. For some types of work, multiple modes are sometimes used in order to minimize the risk. For maximum risk mitigation, a solution should pass through all the different modes. The initial search for a new solution would be informed by demos. Then a POC could be constructed for one or a couple of candidate solutions. If the risk is particularly high, a pilot would be built to try it out in a real setting. Finally, an implementation project would be made either in a waterfall or iterative fashion. This would be the ideal process to determine the right solution with maximum risk mitigation.

However, working in a public context procurement and other challenges makes that a rare occurrence. In many cities, it is considered favoritism of a vendor to do a POC before a procurement. Even demos can be problematic if information about the future project is shared with the vendor in advance of a public tender. Similarly, iterative projects, even if they are most effective, can be problematic since the deliverables are not specified in advance. If it is a capital investment, budget authorities typically want to know very precisely what the investment results in. There are ways around these things. For example, a public tender could call for a POC or a pilot to be milestones. If they are not met, the rest of the contract is not given. A project can also have fixed deliverables but work on them in an iterative fashion. This is one place where smart city technology meets the political realities, and new ways of engagement have to be thought of.

Engagement models

There are different ways to engage with stakeholders to work on smart city technology. It is never something a city can do in isolation. Sometimes the engagement with external partners is minimal as in the case of in-house development; in other cases, it is substantial as is the case with university collaborations.

Traditionally, there were just two ways technology would become implemented in a city: in-house development or procurement from an external partner. These are well tested and still serve the bulk of implementation of city technology, but they are also having some shortcomings. First of all, it is a one-way interaction from city administration to residents. The city comes up with an idea, decides what it needs, and either develops the solution itself or describes what it wants and procures it from a vendor. Second, in this model, all innovation has to come from inside the city administration. While there are innovative individuals working for the city, a good case could be made that important ideas could also be conceived by stakeholders outside the administration. Third, residents, interest groups, and other organizations that have an interest in the city are left out of the equation and are only asked when there is an election cycle. We should therefore expand the view of how smart city technologies can be developed and implemented.

In house – This refers to the city's own IT or technology departments. These are direct hires that work on a particular aspect of technology. The advantage of in-house development is that the developers and engineers working on the solutions acquire a significant domain knowledge and understanding of the problem area. They are able to engage to develop optimal solutions and can also challenge ideas. This model works well for areas where there is significant volume and a stable platform to work on. If the kind of work that needs to get done is fairly similar for years, this is the preferred model. If the city, for example, has to continuously mount new traffic cameras and change existing ones, it makes sense to develop in-house competences since this is similar work that requires a lot of practical expertise. The drawback for this model is that it is not well suited for adopting new technologies since this requires continuous focus and time spent on following the market and developing new competences. While this is possible, and I have seen examples of this, it is rare and an exception.

Procurement – This is the option cities take most often when a new technology has to be implemented. It takes advantage of the market that exists for specialized skills and technologies. When something needs to be implemented that is not part of the existing in-house competences, looking for external partners that have done this for other customers is an option. An example could be if the city wants to implement intelligent electricity meters. This is rarely something that in-house teams have expertise in doing, and consequently procuring it from an external partner is a viable option. The caveat here is not to be dependent on the external vendor. Often initial implementation contracts develop into de facto in-house teams but are paid at external contractor rates. This has every possibility of being just as efficient as an in-house model but comes with a price tag several times higher. Also, knowledge is not being embedded in the organization.

Sponsored – In various circumstances, vendors will sponsor an engagement. Sometimes it is because they want to showcase new solutions, and sometimes, they do it simply to give back to the cities. It is typically challenging to do this from a legal perspective, since this can quickly develop into something resembling corruption or favoritism. That does not mean it is impossible or something that should not be done. Vendors have a lot to offer, and their motives are not always nefarious. This model is well suited for engagements where learning is the main focus such as demos and POCs. Often vendors will also sponsor various kinds of training, which is another important way for the city to learn about new technologies. The vendor-sponsored engagements should be clearly delimited in terms of solution and time. If the engagement becomes one where a solution is offered and continues to be used for real business processes without an endpoint, it should be a cause for concern. Depending on the extent of the collaboration, it may also be a good idea to have a legal agreement on IP and NDAs in place.

Public-private partnerships – Sometimes vendors or other private organizations take the collaboration to a higher level than the vendor sponsored. This is a special case that has a lot of potential for cities to develop new innovative solutions. It requires a clear focus on what the partnership should entail in order to be successful. These are good for POCs and pilots where new solutions have to be developed. There are examples where vendors have standard partner programs that cities can elect to participate in, and there are also more ad hoc partnerships. There are also examples of organizations that are formed with the purpose of fostering public-private engagements. These can be sponsored jointly. Examples of this are city tech labs and various forms of startup incubators and test sites. This is an emerging model of engagement that creates a space for smart city technologies to develop. It can be very efficient. The downside is that it is only part of the full picture. If there is no one on the city side that is ready to take on the innovations, it is just a cosmetic thing that makes politicians look innovative. Thought should be given to how the products from the public-private partnerships could be used.

Hackathons – A popular model of engagement that brings the city closer to its residents is hackathon. A hackathon is an attempt at creating a solution given a number of constraints within a limited period of time, such as an afternoon or evening. Some cities do this to get inspiration for possible new solutions. This is a good way to harness the creativity of the city and find out what sentiments are prevalent. The downside is that it is still a tech elite that shows up at the hackathons. Also, very few if any ideas ever mature into working solutions. The purpose of the hackathons should be clear. If the city expects new ideas to be implemented, there should be a process for how that should be done.

Civic groups – This is the only mode of engagement that is 100% initiated from outside the city. This is why it is often overlooked. There are frequently residents that burn for a cause and start a group that works with technology to improve this from a grassroots perspective. The city can choose to ignore it, but it is a great source of inspiration that may spark lasting change making the city smarter. In contrast to the hackathon, which is a one-off type of thing, the civic technology groups have a lasting organization and work on things they feel the city does not do well enough currently. This is all the more reason for the city to be attentive and supportive. These groups typically don't need help, but the city is in a unique position to aid and learn from their work. The challenge here is that these are in their nature special interest groups that were not democratically elected or appointed. So it may be limited by how much of the city's budget can be allocated toward supporting these types of engagement. That said, they often revolve around common local issues, for example, with the environment or safety. These will often align with established political goals and policies.

University collaboration – Larger cities around the world often have one or more universities close to them. Some are public, some are private, but regardless of that university collaborations are a special model of engagement since universities have particular interests that differ from other types of organizations. A university has a lot of resources when it comes to developing new and innovative smart city solutions. They are naturally always interested in new knowledge and in testing out ideas in the real world, but they are also very interested in creating job opportunities for their students. Universities often look at city partnerships either as paid research, publication potential, or opportunities for students to get practical experience that will qualify them for a job after graduation. If either of these is not the case, the collaboration will be hard to establish. Universities have their own agendas and will not act as the R&D unit for a city. This is why it is important to engage and explore synergies between the two. One thing to be aware of here is that universities are not typically going to be concerned with the practical applicability of their work, but on the other hand, the amount of expertise and brain power they employ is something that is virtually impossible to find on the market. Universities are great for innovation and transformative ideas. For a visualization of the properties of different engagement models of working (see Figure 6-4).

Innovative potential

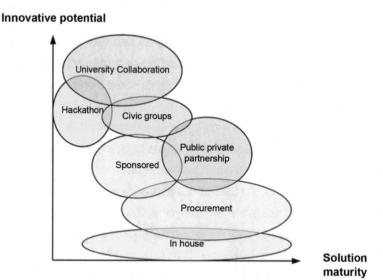

Figure 6-4. *Innovation potential of different engagement models*

Implementing smart city technologies

As we saw previously, smart city technology comes in different types and can be implemented in different ways. In order to be successful with smart city initiatives, it is necessary for a city to understand where it is and where it wants to be on the technology adoption curve. When technology implementations are being considered, their respective position on the technology adoption curve should be matched against the city's.

It is not a good idea for a laggard city to engage in bleeding edge projects. The probability of success will be low because it takes a special way of management and risk tolerance to be successful with that. There is also a good chance that employees will not feel confident when they suddenly have to do a lot of unknown tasks. A city that is just getting ready to move some things off the mainframe may not be an ideal candidate for a block chain implementation.

Conversely, cities that are innovators may not have motivation to implement technologies that provide only incremental gains. They will lose the motivation of their employees who are motivated by trying new things. If they primarily use the newest open source technologies, an ERP implementation is probably not going to energize anyone.

Remember that an adopter category has deep roots in an organization since the organization attracts more people of the same kind. There is an inertia which is very real and must be managed.

Cities that are in the last half of the innovation curve should try to look for technologies that are in the same space, that is, solutions that have many existing implementations among their peers. That does not mean innovation cannot occur, but it needs to be more focused and selective.

Attention should be given to how smart city innovation is done. There are many more engagement models than the traditional in house or procurement that could be explored. Depending on the risk, different stages of a solution could be chosen. Different engagement models fit the different modes of working better (see Table 6-2). For example, university collaborations lend themselves very well to experimental types of work and not maintenance. Conversely, in-house teams are not ideal for truly experimental work. The different engagement models are good to think about how to develop the technology that the future city needs.

Table 6-2. *Engagement models for different modes of working*

Type	BAU	Maintenance	Modernization	Net New	Experimental
In-house	+++	+++	+++	++	
Procurement	+	+	++	+++	
Sponsored					+
Hackathons					++
Civic groups					++
Public-private partnerships				++	++
University collaboration					+++

Solution spotlights

100 Resilient Cities

100 Resilient Cities (100RC) is an organization consisting of 100 cities. It is sponsored by The Rockefeller Foundation and aims to help cities around the world become more resilient to the environmental and social challenges that face them. The organization defines resilience as the ability for cities to overcome shocks (earthquakes, volcanic eruptions, floodings) and stresses (unemployment, pollution, crime). 100RC does this by supporting cities to establish Chief Resilience Officers, develop resilience strategies, and work together to find solutions for resilience challenges. One of the tools 100RC uses is a multiday workshop called a CoLab. The CoLab is a facilitated workshop that helps elicit solutions to problems. Examples have been water supply and earthquakes. In New York, we hosted a CoLab focused on how data could help cities become more resilient. 100 Resilient Cities works with specialists and produces research

based on reporting from the cities. By sharing across multiple cities with similar issues, 100 Resilient Cities allows them to improve. This would be very hard for any city in isolation to orchestrate.

Waze Connected Citizens

Waze is a company owned by Google that specializes in traffic information. Based on users using their app, they can guide them real time through the fastest route to their destination. Users report accidents and other traffic-related information. One of the biggest challenges for drivers and consequently for Waze is street closures and construction. In order to get information from cities on this, Waze created the Connected Citizens Program where participating cities can get close to real-time information on accidents, jams, and traffic speeds in return for sharing information about street closures and construction. The traffic information would be very difficult for cities to produce by themselves, and Waze would not be able to know about street closures and construction work until they have already started. This is a good example of how a public-private partnership can exploit mutual benefits.

BetaNYC

BetaNYC is a civic group that aims to improve the life of New Yorkers through technology and data. They work to empower citizens to use technology and data to improve the lives of New Yorkers and create a more inclusive government. The organization was founded in 2008 and has been a vocal influence on NYC politics inspiring several pieces of legislation. A primary focus is open data, and a close cooperation exists between BetaNYC and the NYC Open Data team. This is an example of how a civic group can inspire and effect positive change when the city is open to their input.

Summary

In order to build smart solutions, cities have to engage with stakeholders supplying technology. Some consideration should go into what technologies and what mix of stakeholders should be chosen.

All technologies are diffused into the market. This is described by the technology adoption curve. Some organizations are naturally inclined to adopt new innovations, and some are skeptical of anything new. Both attitudes belong to the minority, while most are somewhere in the middle leaning either way. Any technology is somewhere on the technology adoption curve. For optimal use, it is important to match the technology with the type of organization.

Adopting new technology is associated with its own risk-reward profile. Depending on this profile, the project will have to be approached differently. There are a number of standard types of work going from low risk to high in any city: business as usual, maintenance, modernization, Net New, and experimental.

Similarly, there are different ways of working: demos, proof of concept, and pilots work as tests of the viability of a new solution, while waterfall and iterative development are the two main modes of implementing new solutions. Understanding what modes of work are effective for which types of work is important.

A city will rarely implement solutions in isolation. Consequently, it has to think about ways to engage stakeholders. Such types of engagement include procurement, sponsored work, public-private partnerships, university collaborations, and more. These all have their own innovative potential and expected solution maturity.

It is important to understand how a city's adoption category matches the technologies it is seeking to implement. Innovation-adverse cities do not benefit from trying to adopt bleeding edge technologies. Further, certain modes of working are better suited to some types of work than others.

PART II

Toward smarter cities

CHAPTER 7

Architect with imagination: Could payphones show the way in an emergency?

Most cities are not greenfield operations that are built from a clean slate like Songdo or Masdar. Most cities are not Versailles that has the luxury of infinite budgets, possibilities, and space. Most cities are like Paris, built according to the way of the pack donkey, in ad hoc and semi-planned fashion through centuries of shifting styles and preferences. The cities we are going to live in in the future are already there with living breathing humans, who depend on them to supply them with basic needs every day. Consequently, our efforts to make them smarter must to a great extent depend on how we modernize them. Just as our cities' infrastructure and buildings need constant renovation, our IT legacy systems need the same modernization effort. In this chapter, we will look at how to make the best of architecting with imagination in this constant process of modernization.

© Anders Lisdorf 2020
A. Lisdorf, *Demystifying Smart Cities*, https://doi.org/10.1007/978-1-4842-5377-9_7

I find the work of Danish architect Bjarke Ingels inspiring. His work includes 2 World Trade Center, Google's Mountain View campus, and LEGO's new headquarters, and it always stretches the boundaries of the possible. For example, faced with a simple renovation project of an old power plant in Copenhagen, Ingels imagined including an idyllic ski slope and making the power plant's chimney puff smoke rings. As Ingels puts it: "Architecture is the fiction of the real world."

But buildings rarely exist in isolation; they are usually part of a city. Ingels continues: "The city is never complete. It has a beginning but no end. It's a work in progress always waiting for new scenes to be added and new characters to move in." While Ingels is talking about real-world brick-and-mortar buildings and other constructions, there is no reason why this would not also apply to IT architecture and the development of smart cities.

This quote also applies to any city. There will always be a technology landscape, and it is always a work in progress. You will never finish and be able to say, "Finally it is here: the smart city." The only thing you can do is to manage the change in a more or less efficient way. When we create the IT architectures of smart cities, we are in essence turning the fiction of user stories and personas into new scenes and characters of this ever-evolving city. Our architectures will be evaluated on whether real characters will inhabit and thrive in the structures we create. Will our designs become like the Chinese ghost town of Ordos that no one inhabits or the smooth coordination of the Tokyo subway that millions of people thrive in day after day?

Just like the buildings and towns we create will only be successful if they become livable by the people they are meant to support, the smart city solutions we build will have to fulfill the functions of the users and surrounding systems.

Typically, we will ask people what they want and document this as requirements, user stories, or use cases. This is all well, but if Ingels had gone out and asked the people of my home town of Copenhagen what they wanted, we would have gotten more of the same apartment blocks and villas that already saturate the city. There would be no power plant with a ski slope simply because people would never have thought about that. If Steve Jobs and Henry Ford had just settled for what people wanted, we would still be speaking in Nokia phones hacking away at clunky black computers and riding in shiny horse-drawn carriages. We cannot expect our users, customers, or politicians to have the imagination. This is something we have to supply and inject into the smart city planning process.

The real frontier for smart cities is imagination. We need to be able to imagine all the things that the requirements and user stories don't tell; we need to be able to be bold and create solutions that no one ever asked for. This is difficult for multiple reasons. First of all, success is usually measured by how well a solution solves the requirements put in front of the architect. That means there is little incentive to do anything more. Second, it is often difficult to gauge what would be needed in the future. Third, there is a tendency toward best practice and existing patterns, which does not further innovative solutions.

However, these obstacles to imagination can be overcome. As Ingels has shown, it is sometimes possible to cover all the basic requirements, in a cost-effective way that does the same or better than traditional solutions. The same is the case for smart city solutions.

Modernizing legacy systems

A big part of making cities smarter, if not the biggest part, is modernizing legacy systems, whether they are signals in the subway, traffic monitoring and control, or regular data center upgrade and maintenance.

This is the type of work we saw previously as migration and maintenance. A migration is rarely a one-to-one migration but will typically include some degree of new functionality as well.

We need to think about the possibilities available to us today and imagine how we would solve the problems that legacy technologies solved in the past given our current technology. We can, in fact, turn fiction into fact; sometimes we just have to be bold and let go of habitual thinking.

A real-world example of legacy modernization

This approach is exactly the one New York took with the LinkNYC kiosks, which we saw in Chapter 2. The city was full of legacy technology in the shape of payphones. It was expensive to maintain them, and they did not support the need they had before people started using cell phones. In a bold move, the city called for rethinking the payphone to fit modern needs like Wi-Fi and cell phone recharging while maintaining the basic functionality of the payphone such as being able to call 911. The result is exactly the stretch of imagination we need to make our cities smarter. The Link kiosks not only do these things but are also able to signal evacuation routes, monitor pollution, and act as a flexible billboard for the city to communicate information. The Link franchise is private and has been adopted in cities such as London, Philadelphia, and Chicago. At the outset, it was still just a legacy system modernization effort. This is an example of what happens when we architect with imagination.

How to architect with imagination

When we modernize and build new systems, there are a couple of things we can do in order to stimulate imagination.

If we modernize a legacy system or reengineer an existing business process, we need to think about what is possible today as opposed to when the legacy solution was built. What technological advances have we seen? We should make sure to fulfill these general criteria. The solution should do the same as today, better at a cheaper price. We also have to look out for superfluous features and not be blinded by how the solutions have been implemented in the past.

164

Recommendations

"The system should do the same as today" – While this is the starting point, it is important to understand that this must not be taken literally. It has to support the same functions and processes but not necessarily in the same way. This is an important point in order to imagine a smarter solution.

If we take the LinkNYC example, the function was for people to call others and call 911. But rather than making a digital payphone, New York decided to imagine other ways to support the same capability. Since things had changed and people now had cell phones themselves, the best way to support the basic function of making it possible to contact others was to provide a charger if their phone was dead and Wi-Fi so that online resources like email and calls could be used. At the same time, the Link kiosks were fitted with a phone to place emergency calls. In this way, we imagined different ways of doing the same as today.

"Make the new solution better" – Thinking about how we can do it better is the most crucial point in architecting with imagination. If we don't think about doing it better, we will end up with a shiny carbon fiber horse-drawn carriage with Ferrari wheels and shiny hubcaps. This is where we have to imagine how things could be different with current technology. This is where civic groups, hackathons, innovation challenges, and startup incubators can help. These are important sources of imagination for the smart city. Vendors are also potentially sources of inspiration, but the result may be more variable since their interests may not be aligned with the city's interests.

Imagining how to do things better involves other types of resources than those who are usually tasked with business as usual and maintenance. Here it is important for the city to facilitate the bridge to these people and organizations because the city is a black box for everything outside. Even if they have ideas, there is no way they know how to get in contact with the relevant units, much less what areas are pain points for the city. A recommendation is to establish liaisons that are tasked with bridging the gap. This person should understand the city's needs and organization and be able to match it to innovation taking place in the city's tech ecosystem.

"Lower the overall cost" – Technology in general should make a business process cheaper when it is looked at holistically. Sometimes this means that some areas will be more expensive but resulting in cost savings in other areas. Leveraging modern technology solutions like cloud computing will be a big part of making the overall cost impact of smart city technologies cheaper, but increased use of open source will also play a role. However, neither option will in and of themselves be cheaper than existing alternatives.

A cloud-based solution can easily be more expensive than a traditional on-premise solution. The reason is that investments are shifted to smaller recurring payments rather than big up-front payments. If the solution is implemented as a traditional on-premise solution, it will typically not be cheaper. The solution has to take into account the price structure and design according to that.

The situation is similar with open source. Many open source offerings have a free version that is very difficult to work with. Developers don't have the possibility to get support like traditional vendor supported solutions. Luckily there are vendors that offer this support and offer standardized versions and additional proprietary features. Quickly, you can end up paying the same as the cost savings that seemed apparent to the open source vendor or the additional resources you have to hire to make it work. However, compared to the incumbents in the enterprise software market, it should be straightforward to provide a cheaper solution.

"Decide if the system should continue to do this going forward" – Often there is legacy functionality that has become naturally obsolete. If there is a solution that sends operational reports to matrix printers in all major offices, this is a good time to stop and reflect on whether the solution should do this in the new version. A hard look is often needed

when we modernize or reengineer business processes and solutions.
Chances are that some functions are no longer needed. It is important to
keep a lookout for these because every function adds to the complexity
and maintenance of the whole solution. The more focused the solution is
on solving the real problems, the better.

**"Decide if the system needs to continue to do what it does in the
same way"** – Reflecting on what a system is doing is almost an existential
exercise but one that needs to be done. Functionality and processes may
seem strange and prove superfluous. It could be due to technological or
other constraints when it was built.

What we need to focus on is the functional or qualitative effect. Rather
than copying how the system does it, we have to reflect on what it needs to
do and imagine the most optimal way in the current context.

The LinkNYC example shows that the most efficient way to make
people able to make a phone call would be to supply them power and
connection to their own devices, because now almost everyone has a
phone. We need to take a holistic look at the context as it is now, not how it
was many years ago when the system was initially built.

"Consider what the system could do in the future" – Keep an eye out
for opportunities that present themselves with rethinking the architecture
and the possibilities of modern technologies. To continue on our example
with the LinkNYC kiosks, we saw that it was possible to add screens
to the payphone substitute. These screens could be used for showing
relevant information for the city's residents like city-sponsored events. It
also found use as showing critical information in emergencies. This was
demonstrated in the steam pipe explosion that happened on Manhattan
in July 2018. The Link kiosks displayed evacuation routes for people in the
vicinity of the explosion.

Being open minded and having a view to related use cases is important
to spot these opportunities. This may take a bit of work around the
institutional silos if such exist, but it carries with it great potential. In order
to be open to such opportunities, it is important to be aware of what is going

on and what solutions are being worked on. The city should find ways to facilitate these serendipitous encounters, for example, by creating cross-organizational forums where solutions are being presented or reviewed. It could also be done by making sure that a group of people are responsible for and have knowledge about cross-organizational opportunities.

Summary

Most cities are not greenfield operations that are built from a clean slate. They are already there, and our efforts to make them smarter must to a great extent depend on how we modernize them. Just as our cities' infrastructure and buildings need constant renovation, our IT legacy systems need the same modernization effort. Taking the lead of Bjarke Ingels, we are encouraged to reimagine the possible rather than reproducing the legacy in a new technology.

This was what New York City did with the LinkNYC kiosks that offer charging, wifi, and information screens to the public as a replacement for the old payphones. They can even show the way in case of an emergency. This is the kind of imagination we need to get the maximum benefit from smart cities solutions. We have to start architecting with imagination.

In order to do that, we need to ask ourselves a number of key questions like whether the system should do what it does today and whether it has to be done in the same way and can we do it in a different and more cost-efficient way? Often legacy systems were built according to technological constraints that existed at the time of development. It is important not to replicate these constraints if they no longer exist in the technology landscape. Similarly, the usage patterns and context may have changed as was the case with payphones. These considerations should go hand in hand with imagining how we can do something more and better. This way we can turn boring and uninspiring modernization efforts into opportunities for implementing solutions that make the city a better place to live.

CHAPTER 8

Make innovation a habit: Why most innovation is like low-fat yogurt

The challenge of sustaining innovation

Innovation is like a slim waistline, good grades, and a good marriage, something everybody wants but few want to do the necessary work to attain. We often look toward innovation leaders in awe like we look at movie stars or fashion models. We want to look like them, but it takes a workout regime of several hours a day six days a week and a controlled diet. And yes, that means no cake.

Frequently though this point does get through and results in a diet. This will last 6–12 weeks. Hopefully you saw results and were able to admire your slim waistline. However, once the diet stops, everything is back to normal. Now you can snack and chill on the couch watching Netflix because you have a slim(mer) waistline. Within another 6–12 weeks, you are back to where you started.

© Anders Lisdorf 2020
A. Lisdorf, *Demystifying Smart Cities*, https://doi.org/10.1007/978-1-4842-5377-9_8

Innovation often follows a similar trajectory. Most organizations value innovation and will sponsor it. They will make an innovation challenge. Maybe they will invite startups to collaborate on a theme of interest and write press releases and have photo opportunities. This feels good, and it feels right, just like the diet.

Unfortunately, just like the diet, once the spotlight is gone, we are back to normal. Only this time it is with a vengeance because now we will feel justified in continuing our old bad habits, because we have just shown that we are innovative, right? Paradoxically, many innovation efforts end up reinforcing traditional thinking because to the organization they see themselves as innovative due to the innovative events and initiatives they have sponsored; all the while, they carry on doing exactly what they have always done.

Innovation is doing something in a new way that we have not done before; however, humans are psychologically inclined to do exactly what they are used to doing. We want to sit at the same desk or the same table at the canteen and drink the same beverages even though it would be better for us to mix it up. We might find new friends or interesting conversations and may even identify tastier beverages. In addition, our preferences are not always good for us. We have a preference for rest and fat and sugary foods (which do not lead to a slim waistline). This is often overlooked in discussions of innovation: nobody really wants innovation; they just want the benefits of innovation and to continue doing what they are used to while claiming they are innovative.

The habit loop

In order to harvest the fruits of innovation, we need to realize that it takes discipline and determination and a long-term focus. Like movie stars and models, it requires us to make a change of habit to enjoy the benefits of innovation. This is the subject of Charles Duhigg's book *The Power of*

Habit. In it he describes exactly what this entails. Duhigg finds that habits can be understood according to a habit loop. Let us consider the example of the habit of taking a snack with your coffee. In this case, the habit loop consists of the following:

1) **Cue** – This is what triggers the habit. Having a coffee at Michelle's Cafe is the cue.

2) **Routine** – Is the actual behavior associated with the habit. In our example, it is choosing that innocent-looking donut with pink frosting.

3) **Reward** – The positive emotion of performing the routine. In our example, it is the bliss of the sugar high and how the taste of that donut melts together with the double-shot oat milk latte with a touch of cinnamon.

If we want to change this habit, we have to do a bit of habit reengineering. We need to intervene at the cue and introduce a healthier routine that similarly carries a reward.

In order to get into the habit of innovation, we also need to reengineer our routines: the following is necessary in order to make lasting changes. First, we need to identify the habit we want to change with innovation. Do we want to be more innovative in our product development, hiring, or communication, for example? Let's say we want to build more innovative solutions in our city. Most solutions are implemented with projects. There will always be more projects than the city is able to fund and run, so someone needs to make a decision about what projects to run at some point. Let us look at how we can make more innovative projects a habit:

Cue – The project initiation decision is the cue for our habit. If this is a portfolio review board, then we need to intervene here. If it is senior management, then this is where we start. Somewhere the decision to start a project is made, and we need to find it.

Routine – Here we have to understand the existing habitual behavior that we want to change. How are projects being chosen today? Why these projects? Who is involved and in what capacity? Next, we have to do our habit reengineering and insert a routine that is consistent with our intent of being innovative. We know that we should look at new technologies or alternate ways of thinking about the problem, but how do we do this in practice? If we already score projects on different parameters, we could introduce an innovation score. We could also allocate a fixed amount of resources for innovative projects. Creating a special innovation team is a bad way since this isolates the innovative behavior from influencing the way the organization as a whole works. We should therefore look at subtle ways of changing the existing routines. This is also why most diets are unsuccessful: the amount of change is too massive and will feel alien. We are therefore looking at minimal changes similar to substituting our delicious donut with an apple. Examples could be to let employees spend time on innovative projects that would usually be considered a waste of time or circulate them through an innovation lab.

Reward – For the habit-forming process, this is the most important point. It is not enough to have a ceremony after an innovation challenge and issue press releases. The reward needs to come consistently and as a product of the routine described previously. This is where it gets difficult, because most innovations fail or are not immediately valuable due to the nature of innovations. Remember from the previous discussion that with high reward also comes high risk. If the organization usually punishes failures, this is an immediate place to intervene. Risk taking should be rewarded even when it fails if the organization wants to harvest the rewards of innovations. Based on my experience trying to create innovative solutions in many different industries, this is typically where innovation fails because decision makers are not really ready to reward outlandish and speculative ideas. The old adage that "No one ever got fired for buying IBM" (and you could add "even if they should have") applies as a general rule here – because failed projects are one of the things that will get you fired. The incentive structures have to be aligned so as to reward innovation for it to ever take hold in an organization.

Avoiding low-fat yogurt innovation

Today innovation is too often treated like low-fat yogurt. You eat it in the morning, and then in the evening you feel justified in lounging on the couch with a bag of chips and soda, because, you know, you can convince yourself that you have a healthy diet. If you want to become innovative, you need to figure out first what that means to you and specifically what areas of your value stream are impacted. Then you need to do some analysis and reengineering, and most of all you need to be consistent in rewarding innovative behavior. If you are not willing to put in the hours in the gym, it is much better for you to not do anything and realize that you are not innovative. If you are late majority or laggards (as we saw in Chapter 6), innovation is dangerous for you, and you should not experiment with it. It will sap the powers of those trying to innovate and will divert attention from things that are considered valuable in the organization.

CHAPTER 9

Build the data refinery: Because cities run on data

From raw data to useful information

"Data is the new oil!" Mathematician and IT architect Clive Humby seems to have been the first to coin the phrase in 2006 where he helped Tesco develop from a fledgling UK retail chain to an intercontinental titan that rivals the likes of Walmart and Carrefour, through the use of data. This was done with the Tesco loyalty program that pioneered offers targeted to particular segments. Several people have reiterated the concept subsequently. But the realization did not really hit prime time until *The Economist* in May 2017 claimed that data had surpassed oil as the most valuable resource.

It is safe to say that cities in general and smart cities in particular run on data. Without data there is no smart city. Consequently, it is crucial that we build solutions for optimal utilization of this data.

However, data is not just out there and up for grabs. Just like you have to figure out how to get oil out of the ground first, data poses similar challenges: you need to get it out of computer systems or devices first. When you do get the oil out of the ground, it is still virtually useless.

© Anders Lisdorf 2020
A. Lisdorf, *Demystifying Smart Cities*, https://doi.org/10.1007/978-1-4842-5377-9_9

Crude oil is just a nondescript blob of black goo. Getting the oil is just a third of the job. This is why we have oil refineries. Oil refineries turn crude oil into valuable and consumable resources like gas or diesel or propane. It splits the raw oil into different substances that can be used for multiple different products like paint, asphalt, nail polish, basketballs, fishing boots, guitar strings, and aspirin. This is awesome; can you imagine a world much less a party without guitar strings, fishing boots, and aspirin? That would be like Harry Potter without the magic...

Similarly, even if we can get our hands on it, raw data is completely useless. If you have ever glanced at a web server log, a binary data stream, or telemetry data, you can relate to the analogy of crude oil as a big useless blob of black goo. All this data does not mean anything in itself. Getting the raw data is of course a challenge in some cases, but making it useful is a completely different story. That is why we need to build data refineries: systems that turn the useless raw data into components that we can build useful data products from.

The structure of the data refinery

While working on modernizing data services at the city of New York, we worked to design and architect such a data refinery. The "Data as a Service" program was the effort to build this refinery to turn raw data into valuable and consumable services to be used by city agencies, residents, and the rest of the world. There are multiple data sources in systems of record, registers, logs, official filings and applications, inspections, and hundreds of thousands of devices. Only a fraction of this data was even available. When it was available, it was hard to discover and use. The purpose of Data as a Service was to make all the hidden data available and useful. We wanted to turn all this raw data into valuable and consumable data services.

A typical refinery processes crude oil. This is done through a series of distinct process phases and results in distinct products that can be used for different purposes. The purpose of the refinery is to break down the crude oil to useful by-products. The data refinery has five capability domains we need to manage in order to break the raw data down into useful data assets (see Figure 9-1).

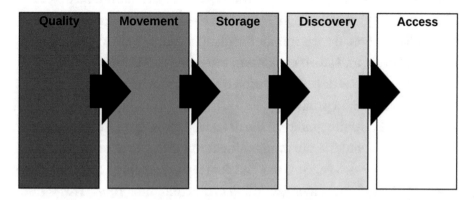

Figure 9-1. *Capability domains in the data refinery*

- **Quality** is about the character and validity of the data assets.

- **Movement** is how we transfer and transform data assets from one place to another.

- **Storage** deals with how we retain data assets for later use.

- **Discovery** has to do with how we locate the data assets we need.

- **Access** deals with how we allow users and other solutions to interact with data assets.

Let us look at each of these in a bit more detail.

Quality

The first capability domain addresses the quality of the data. The raw data is initially of low quality. It may be a stream of bits or characters, telemetry data, logs, or CSV files. The first thing to think about in any data refinery is how to assess and manage the quality of the data. We want to understand and control the quality of data. We want to know how many data objects are there, if they are of the right format, or if they are corrupted. Simple descriptive reports like the number of distinct values, type mismatch, number of nulls, and so on can be very revealing and important when considering how the data can be used by other systems and processes. This is known as data profiling.

Once we know the quality of the data, we may want to intervene and do something about it. Data preparation formats the data from its initial raw form. It may also validate that the data is not corrupted and can delete, insert, and transform values according to preconfigured rules. This is the first diagnostic and cleansing of the data in the data refinery.

Once we have the initial data objects lined up in an appropriate format, master data management (MDM) is what allows us to work proactively and reactively on improving the data. With MDM we will be able to uniquely identify data objects across multiple different solutions and format them into a common semantic model. MDM enables an organization to manage data assets and produce golden records, identify and eliminate duplicates, and control what data entities are valid and invalid.

The quality domain has to diagnose and manage the quality of data. A number of capabilities are needed to do this such as data profiling, data preparation, and MDM.

Data movement

Once we have made sure that we can manage the quality of the data, we can proceed to the next phase. Here we will move and transform the data into more useful formats. We may, however, need to move data differently according to how it will be stored and used. Sometimes it is all well to move it once a day, week, or even month, but more often we want the data immediately.

Batch is movement and transformation of large volumes of data from one form and place to another. A typical batch program is executed on a schedule and goes through a sequence of processing steps that transforms the data from one form into another. It can range from simple formatting changes and aggregations to complex machine learning models.

When files need to be moved securely between different points without any transformation, a managed file transfer solution is needed. This is typically accessed by applications, but a portal also allows users to upload or download the file. This is to be distinguished from document sharing sites like SharePoint, Dropbox, Box, and Google Docs where the purpose is for human end users to share files with other humans and typically cooperate on authoring them.

The Enterprise Service Bus (ESB) is a data processing paradigm that lets different applications interact with each other through messaging. A message is a small discrete unit of data that can be routed, transformed, distributed, and otherwise processed as part of the information flow in the Service Bus. This is what we use when systems need to communicate real time across city agencies. It is a centralized orchestration.

Some data is not as nicely and easily managed. We see use cases where the processing can't wait for batch processing and the ESB paradigm does not scale well with high volumes. Real-time stream processing works on data that arrives in continuous streams. It has limited routing and transformation capabilities but is well suited to handle large volumes of data that comes in continuously either to store, process, or forward it.

Depending on the source of data, the data movement domain contains different solutions for processing and moving the data between solutions. Focus should be on selecting the right capability in each particular case.

Storage

Moving the data requires places to move it to. Different ways of storing data have different properties, and we want to optimize the utility by choosing the right way to store the data.

One important way to store data is the Data Warehouse. This is a relational database that contains data prepared for frequent ad hoc analytical access by business users. It can contain pre-aggregated data and calculations that are frequently needed. Schemas are built in advance to address identified reporting needs. The Data Warehouse focuses on centralized storage and consequently data, which has utility across different city agencies.

Whereas Data Warehouses store structured data, a Data Lake is primarily a store for unstructured data (see Chapter 4). The Data Lake is a place to store data first and then think about how to use it later. It is typically designed with different zones within the Data Lake with varying degrees of structure and purpose. There are no generally accepted standards for what zones to include. The following are typical zones that could be considered:

- **The raw zone** is used for landing raw data from the source systems unmodified from the source systems. This could be structured, semi-structured, and unstructured data. Users should not be given access to this zone. For the data to be used, it should be moved to another zone like the analytical, operational, or discovery zone.

- **The analytical zone** has formatted data prepared for analytical use. It is not the same as a Data Warehouse where a lot of thought has been given to how the data is structured. This is a centrally managed area with governance around the data sets that are exposed such as access rights and metadata describing what it is. Here a data asset should exist only in one version sanctioned by the data owner.

- **The discovery zone** is specific to a unit or organization, and users can bring in their own data or create their own versions of data sets. This is not meant for general consumption but is more like a sandbox for data scientists where they can prepare new data sets and make ad hoc experiments. It is the only zone the users have a possibility to create and upload data to.

- **The operational zone** is like a traditional operational data store and is in essence a read replica of an operational database. It is used in order not to unnecessarily affect an operational, transactional database with queries.

- **The archive zone** is where data will be moved when there is no more need to access the data frequently. Consequently, data access can have a long latency period. Archives are typically used in cases where regulatory requirements warrant data to be kept for a specific period of time. This can be used as a generic archive even for solutions that do not have any analytical use cases. Cities used to have real warehouses filled with paper archives that burned down every now and then. The reason for this is that all data has a retention policy that specifies how long

it should be stored. This need is still there when we
digitize data. Consequently, we need to be in complete
control of all data assets' lifecycle, which is what the
archive zone handles.

Data Warehouses are highly tailored constructs that align the
semantics of an organization with source data from multiple systems in a
coherent fashion, but sometimes it is necessary to go straight to the source
systems for data. Typically, we do not want to interfere with operational
systems, and analytical queries can significantly degrade the performance
of a database. In order to support this type of use, we need an operational
data store (ODS) that is essentially a read replica of a source system or at
least the important tables of a source system.

There is always a need to have somewhere to store unspecified files of
any kind be it Excel sheets, documents, images, video, and so on. The file
share is a well-known and multipurpose storage option.

The standard relational database is the workhorse of any city or
other organizations because of its versatility and power. Refined through
decades, the relational database is a first choice for most types of data
storage across use cases.

The storage domain contains different capabilities that are needed to
handle the different requirements for storing data. Depending on the use
case, the optimal form should be identified.

Discovery

Now that we have ways to control the quality, we can move the data and
store it; we also need to be able to discover it. Data that cannot be found is
useless. Therefore, we need to supply a number of capabilities for finding
the data we need.

If the user is in need of a particular data asset, search is the way to locate
it. Based on familiar query functions, the user can use single words or strings.

We all know this from online search engines. The need is the same here: to be able to intelligently locate the right data asset based on an input string.

When the user does not know exactly what data assets he or she is looking for, we want to be able to supply other ways of discovering data. In a data catalog, the user can browse existing data sources and locate the needed data based on tags or groups. The catalog also allows previews as well as additional metadata about the data source, such as descriptions, data dictionaries, and experts to contact. This is convenient if the user does not already know exactly what data asset is needed.

In some cases, a user knows exactly what subset of data is needed. The data may not all reside in the same place or format. Rather than creating a new source with duplicate data, we want to use data virtualization. By introducing a virtual layer between the user and the data sources, it is possible to create durable semantic layers that remain even when data sources are switched. It is also possible to tailor specific views of the same data source to a particular audience. This way the view of the data will cater to the needs of individual user groups rather than a catch-all lowest common denominator. This is particularly convenient since access to sensitive data is granted on a per-case basis. The data virtualization will make it possible for users to discover only the data they are legally mandated to view.

The discovery domain is about how we discover data. Without being able to find the data we need, all the data in the world would be useless. Depending on the use case, different capabilities need to be in place for the users to discover that data they need.

Access

Now that we are in control of the quality of data, moving and storing it and letting users discover it, we also need to think about how we can let users consume the data. Across the city, there are very different needs for consuming data.

Access by applications is granted through an API and supplies a standardized way for programmatic access by external and internal IT solutions. The API controls ad hoc data access and also supplies documentation that allows developers to interact with the data through a developer portal. Typically, the data elements are smaller and involve a dialogue between the solution and the API.

An end user will sometimes need to query a data source in order to extract a subset of the data. Query allows this form of ad hoc access to underlying structured or semi-structured data sources. This is typically done through SQL. An extension of this is natural language queries through which the user can interrogate a data source through questions and answers. With the advent of colloquial interfaces like Alexa, Siri, and Cortana, this is something we expect to develop further.

End users often need to be able to easily access and collaborate on a document across organizational boundaries and also with users outside the organization. For this purpose, it is necessary to set up a document share that is web based, flexible, and easy to use as a self-service option for end users. This is similar to the file share, but focused on end users and collaboration, where the file share is focused on internal use without any collaboration element.

Notifications are messages that function as triggers from systems that indicate that something has happened or should happen. Other systems can subscribe to notifications and implement adequate responses to them. Similar to streams, they are real time, but contrary to streams, they are not continuous. They also resemble APIs in that it is usually smaller messages but differ in that they implement a push pattern that notifies the target application contrary to the API which is request-response.

Overview of the data refinery

Going back to the five domains of the data refinery that we identified earlier, we can now populate it with a few key capabilities (see Figure 9-2). These capabilities are not exhaustive, and others may be added. It is also not necessary that all of them are needed initially. Typically, a city will already have solutions in place that support some of the capabilities. It is therefore necessary to make an analysis of the maturity of these offerings. In some areas, there are hopefully sufficient solutions in place, while others need attention and yet others are completely lacking. A prioritization should take place for which capabilities are most important to improve, and a roadmap should be developed. The data refinery map is one way to give structure and vision to a gradual improvement in the city's ability to process and manage data.

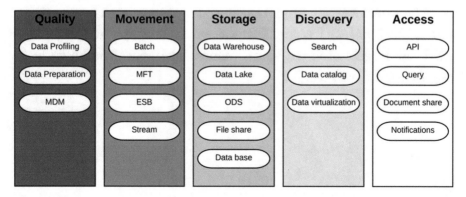

Figure 9-2. *Key capabilities in the five domains of the data refinery*

Strategies for implementing the data refinery

In any city, some of this will already have been built, since processing data is not something new. What we need to do is to modernize existing implementations of the abovementioned capabilities and plan for how to implement the missing ones. This involves a jigsaw puzzle of projects, stakeholders, and possibilities.

Like we saw in Chapter 7, we are rarely working from a greenfield, and there is no multimillion-dollar budget for creating all these interesting new solutions. Rather we have to continuously come up with ways to reach the target incrementally.

This is what we will see and describe as pragmatic idealism in Chapter 11. What is most important is to have a bold and comprehensive vision for where we want to go. The data refinery template serves as the starting point for such a vision. That way we can hold up every project and decision against this target and evaluate how we can continuously progress toward our goal.

Optimize data value, not just data quality: How to avoid another Mars Climate Orbiter disaster

The seven dimensions of data value

It was with great excitement for our exploration of space in general and our red neighbor, Mars, in particular that NASA sent the Mars Climate Orbiter away 20 years ago on December 11, 1998. The orbiter was supposed to study Mars's atmosphere and climate in order to get a better understanding of Martian weather and seasons.

On September 2 the following year at 2 AM Pacific Time, the Orbiter fired its main engine to go into orbit around the planet. But shortly after, contact disappeared. Later investigations revealed that the Orbiter was lost. The reason was that it had entered the atmosphere in a wrong angle and crashed. The root cause for that failure was that one development team had used imperial units (e.g., miles and pounds) and the other the metric

© Anders Lisdorf 2020
A. Lisdorf, *Demystifying Smart Cities*, https://doi.org/10.1007/978-1-4842-5377-9_10

system (e.g., kilometers and kilograms). Thus, our exploration of Mars and
the solar system was halted by something as simple as a data failure.

More than just a key component in space exploration data is the fuel
of our contemporary and future world: our banking system for example
is basically just data. Whereas earlier account balances, stocks, and
transactions were tied to paper documents with seals and signatures, today
they are merely data structures in computer systems. As artificial intelligence
takes over more and more functions from humans, they do so running on
data and their proper functioning depends on it. As more and more aspects
of our lives from taxes to dating and news sources are captured in computer
systems, how we manage and use this data becomes more important.

Data impacts virtually all aspects of our life. Without proper data, our
efforts to leverage artificial intelligence and automating processes and
systems that we depend on will fail. Our future depends crucially on our
ability to produce adequate data.

The problem is that technology professionals today are focused only
on data quality, which is important, but also misses the point, since perfect
quality data still can be insufficient. In the Mars Climate Orbiter example,
there is no indication that data was somehow of bad quality.

We therefore need a more comprehensive way to think about data than
just focusing on data quality. It is necessary to shift the focus to thinking
about data value. Just as the value of things depends on their utility, data
value depends on the degree to which data is fit for purpose.

Here we want to propose seven dimensions of data value that can
help focus our efforts on improving data and making technology solutions
better and more efficient:

- **Consumption** – How data is offered to systems and users

- **Structure** – The format and constitution of data

- **Granularity** – The level of detail available

- **Freshness** – How old the data is

- **Content** – What the data represents

- **Validity** – How accurately the data represents reality

- **Intelligibility** – The degree to which data is
  understandable

In order to build optimal technological solutions, we need to
understand and manage these seven dimensions of data. In the end of
this chapter, we will look at a few ways to improve data value along these
dimensions.

The seven dimensions are divided into two spheres (see Figure 10-1):
data and metadata. The data dimensions relate to properties of the data
itself. This is the actual data that we can read and write. The metadata
dimensions relate to properties about the data. These properties cannot be
seen directly from the data but supplement the data and describes how to
interpret and use the data. Both spheres are equally important in order to
have a holistic concept of data value.

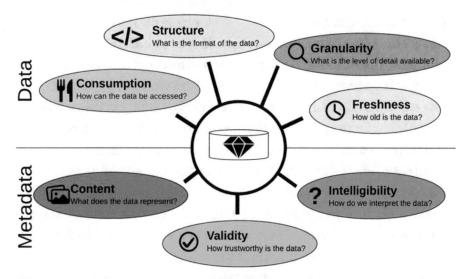

Figure 10-1. *The seven dimensions of data value*

The data sphere

Consumption – "How can the data be accessed?" For many years, the
default answer has been microservices or another type of API as the way to
access data. These are ways to programmatically interact with application
functionality from other applications in a Request-Response type of
interaction. The consuming application calls the API and requests a piece
of data, and the API returns the data. The problem is if you are building a
machine learning solution and need to loop through millions of entities
as part of the process, this may not be the optimal solution. You might just
rather want a file. For an analyst working on a problem, an SQL interface
may be preferable (see Chapter 4). These are some of the considerations
that are relevant to think about when planning out your data offering. The
consumption dimension describes how data should be consumed.

Structure – "What is the format of the data?" From the VSAM days
of the mainframe to the Hadoop age of Parquet, data has always had
a predefined structure. This structure determines how you can access
the data contained in the file. This is true for large files as well as small
messages in JSON or XML. VSAM, Parquet, JSON, and XML are different
file formats. The structure is a key property of how you can work with the
data, since it optimizes for different things. Some formats are optimized
for speed, while others may be optimized for rigor and precision. This has
consequences for the processes that use them. The structure dimension
therefore deals with how processes will typically use the data.

Granularity – "What is the level of detail available?" The level of detail
available can be crucial in some contexts. Granularity can be thought of in
different ways: it may be in terms of time as is the case with how precisely
an observation is captured. This is critical for sporting events like downhill
skiing. It could also be resolution as is the case with the Large Hadron
Collider, the world's largest and most powerful particle accelerator at CERN
in Switzerland, where the granularity level is down to subatomic particles.
In some cases, even the right data can be without value if the granularity is

too high. Think of autonomous vehicles navigating through a city. If they work with maps that are accurate to within a few meters no matter how precise, it might prove fatal. Centimeter-precise maps are needed. The granularity dimension concerns the precision of the data offered.

Freshness – "How old is the data?" From the time of the horseback courier through the carrier pigeon and the telegraph until our modern Internet, the quest for ever more fresh data has driven the technological evolution. In some cases, the speed with which you can get the data is critical and needs to be optimized, such as in high-frequency trading, while in other cases it might be irrelevant as in monthly job reports. Optimizing for speed is costly and highly specialized. Consequently, understanding the need for freshness is important. The freshness dimension describes the time from the occurrence or observation of an event until it is available for consumption.

The metadata sphere

Content – "What does the data represent?" If you don't know what the data is, it is worthless. Describing the data is crucial for its value. A string of values is only valuable if you know what they denote. This is why data dictionaries have been recommended for decades when designing databases. The content of a data asset makes it possible to determine what it can be used for. The content dimension defines what the data is.

Validity – "How trustworthy is the data?" Having data about let's say global warming is only as valuable as the validity of the measurement. This is why extraordinary measures have been taken to prove the validity of the measuring techniques. Any sensor reading is only as good as the sensor's ability to pick up a signal. In some cases, it is necessary to develop ways to prove validity more stringently. When we test solutions, we do so to prove that we can trust the data. It is important to know how valid it is, and this should be described and documented. The validity dimension concerns the certainty with which the data represents something.

Intelligibility – "How do we interpret the data?" Getting from data
to something that makes sense is sometimes a longer journey. One thing
is having the data but understanding it is another. Obviously, encryption
is one way to render data unintelligible; an encryption key is needed.
Sometimes even unencrypted data such as sensor readings may be
unintelligible if you don't know how to read them. But issues surrounding
intelligibility can be even simpler. If we go back to the story at the start
of this chapter, the data scored high on all the previous six dimensions:
it was well formatted, timely, and well understood, but the readings
were understood by one team as metric units and by others as imperial
units. Intelligibility describes the extent to which the nature of the data is
understood.

How to improve data value

Knowing and understanding the different dimensions of data value is only
half the job. It gives us a starting point from which we can now work to
improve the value of our data. In the following are a number of ways to
do that.

Store once/open consumption – Rather than building multiple
parallel solutions for different consumption patterns, one source
should be implemented and consumption built on that same source.
Traditionally, different consumption styles have their own data store like
a Data Warehouse for analytics, a web service for API, and a streaming
platform for real-time data. Instead of building individual siloed data
stores, attention should be given to make these consumption styles rely
on the same store. Today data virtualization and caching tools can go a
long way toward this end. That said it is always a tradeoff between what
dimensions are most important. If freshness is most important, latency is
crucial, and optimized solutions for that should be chosen. Similarly, if one
consumption style dominates, like APIs, a different solution is preferable.

The major benefit of the store once/open consumption architecture is that data consistency is improved, and data lineage transparency is higher.

Persist data in lowest granularity – In traditional business intelligence, attention has been given to finding the right grain for data. This is still important, but first data should be stored in the absolute lowest granularity. If a higher grain is needed, it can easily be aggregated by a subsequent process. The reason for this is that whatever is the current need, the future may require lower granularity, and if this is not even stored, it will be impossible to get to without rebuilding the solution. One example is maps of cities. The granularity of traditional GIS data maps, which is within meters, is fine for most applications like route optimization, GPS services, and putting addresses on a map, but for autonomous vehicles, it is not enough, and centimeter-precise maps need to be developed. This is why the lowest granularity available should be chosen.

Make data discoverable – If no one knows data exists, it is worthless. Making data discoverable and understanding what it represents are crucial for improving the recyclability of data. An alarming amount of work is being done to procure the same data by different teams and projects in most companies around the world, but also cities struggle with knowing what data is available. Especially in moments of crisis, this becomes crucial to saving lives. At a workshop hosted by 100 Resilient Cities and the city of New York, the topic was how we could use data to improve the resilience of our cities. The brainstorming session produced multiple suggestions, but the one with most votes was the data catalog. Making it possible to find the data you need is crucial for realizing the value of data.

Promote data lineage transparency – Data scientists around the world spend an inordinate amount of time and worry about where their data comes from and try to track down all the steps it goes through before it ends up in their data source. This is with good reason since this is crucial to the quality and nature of the data. Promoting data lineage transparency can be solved with tools, but they typically cover only the particular vendor stack. Other ways to promote transparency is through documentation.

For each data set, even a crude sketch of the different steps the data goes through and an architectural drawing that shows the source systems would go a long way.

Real time first – Many processes and use cases do not require data to be real time. The traditional batch approach is fine. This is the case for BI. But when a process like an API suddenly needs data in real time, a new parallel solution has to be built. If transformations take place, differences between the batch and real-time processing could occur. Consequently, it is better to have just one mechanism, since batch can always run on the log of real-time events. Real-time processes also allow us to spot failures faster, so they can be corrected faster.

Improve metadata – The metadata is a product of processes that do not stem from the data itself. Consequently, it can rarely be solved with an automated solution. Rather it needs to be engineered with processes and organizational structures. Testing that data is accurate according to the specified business rules is a way to increase validity. The same is true of testing in labs or through spot tests. Describing the nature of the data such as the units used and properties related to its collection will increase the intelligibility. In New York City, we worked on a project to count vehicles with machine learning algorithms; we were baffled that apparently traffic volume did not pick up until around 10 AM in our data set. When we investigated, eventually we figured out that the timestamp used recorded time in UTC, but New York is UTC-5. Hence 10 AM is really 5 AM Eastern Time. This is a critical piece of metadata to record for the users of the data. With adequate metadata, many misunderstandings and misapplications can be countered.

Manage data structure – Managing the structure of the data is important and the main focus of data quality and master data management initiatives. The structure defines how machines will be able to understand and act on data. Whereas humans are better to spot that an "o" is a typo for a "0," this will completely escape computer systems. Part of managing the structure is also to test that it is fit for purpose, for example, making sure with automated tests that an API format is still consistent after a new version is deployed.

Build a data taxonomy – Part of understanding the content of data is also to understand how it fits into the bigger picture. A taxonomy puts data assets into a system where relations to other data assets can be seen. The Danish Agency for Digitisation has developed an information model that defines all central concepts like buildings, persons, and places. This helps understanding what, for example, a person is in relation to a family or places. But it is important to be clear that taxonomies need not be large all-encompassing conceptual schemes. They can be something as simple as tags. Regardless of method, the important thing here is to be able to map the data asset to the taxonomy.

Optimizing data value with the data value scorecard

We can't rely on a suite of data quality tools to make sure our data is fit for purpose and valuable for the systems and people who will use it. Rather we need to switch to a more holistic view of data that supports different needs. Data is the foundation of our future, whether it be space exploration, public safety, or building equitable, sustainable smart cities. Focusing on the seven dimensions of data value is one way to make sure that our data will also drive our future in optimal ways. To this end, I have developed the data value scorecard which can be found at `www.datavaluescorecard.com`. It is a tool that can help you reflect on the seven dimensions and also identify the gaps in your current data offering (see Figure 10-2).

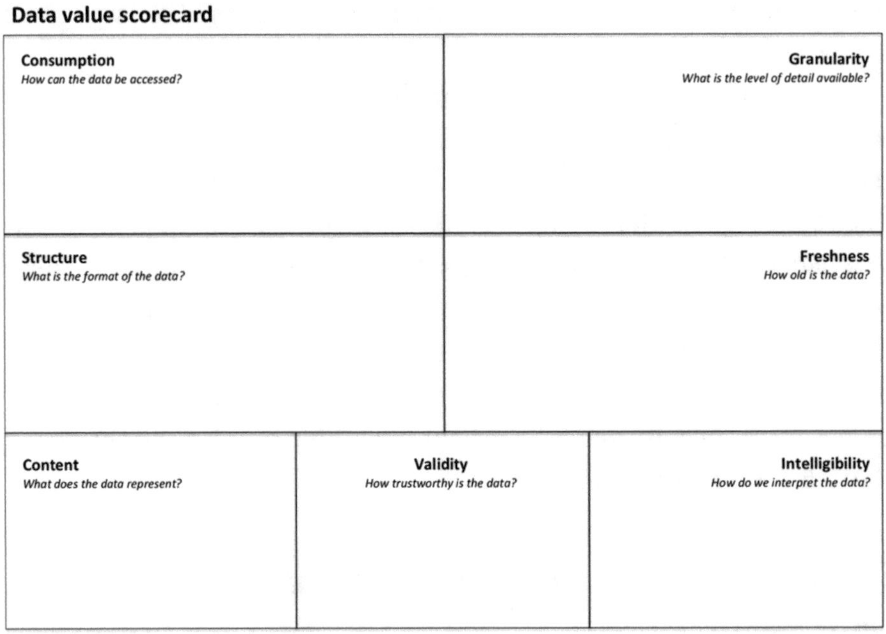

Data value scorecard

Consumption *How can the data be accessed?*		Granularity *What is the level of detail available?*
Structure *What is the format of the data?*		**Freshness** *How old is the data?*
Content *What does the data represent?*	**Validity** *How trustworthy is the data?*	**Intelligibility** *How do we interpret the data?*

Figure 10-2. *The data value scorecard*

One way to use it is to focus on a particular data asset. Then divide each block in two. To the left, you write the current state. To the right, you do research with current or potential users of the data asset in order to determine what their needs are. Write this in the right half of the box. This way you can get an overview of the gap by comparing the left side to the right side of each box. It can also be used to trim the data offering, since some current offerings may not even be needed by users.

CHAPTER 11

Employ pragmatic idealism: Bridging the ivory tower and the trenches

The idealist and the pragmatist realms

Having worked for many years as an enterprise architect, I am not insensitive to the skyward gazes that project managers or developers make when being "assigned" an architect. The architect is frequently perceived as living in an ivory tower of abstraction in perfect disjunction from the real world. At best he is a distraction, at worst a liability for the project to deliver.

The architect sometimes lives in a completely idealized world, and he is tasked with implementing these ideals. However, often this fails precisely because the ideals rarely conform to the reality. The architect fails to appreciate what in military parlance is sometimes referred to as "the facts on the ground." He is too often the desktop general, an idealist.

© Anders Lisdorf 2020
A. Lisdorf, *Demystifying Smart Cities*, https://doi.org/10.1007/978-1-4842-5377-9_11

There are some symptoms of an idealist realm that can be spotted in an organization:

- "There is a guideline for that."

- Templates for any occasion.

- "We have it documented in our Enterprise Architecture tool, any other questions?"

- More than 3% of the IT organization are architects.

- CMMI level 5 is viewed as the minimum requirement for doing any kind of serious work.

Now consider the architect's counterparts: project managers, developers, or system administrators who just want to get the job done in a predictable way or any way really. These guys live "the facts on the ground." They know all the peculiarities of the environment or system being worked on. They are pragmatists.

The symptoms of a pragmatist realm are the following:

- "If something breaks, we fix it so we can get back to our coffee break."

- Upgrade what is already in place when it has run out of support (urgency promotes action).

- Always enhance existing functionality, it already works!

- New technology is like the flu; it will pass, no need to get it.

- A big pot of Status Quo (not the band) with a dash of Not-invented-here.

The pragmatist wanders from compromise to compromise. He is running from battle to battle. This will rarely win the war.

It seems that we are left between a rock and a hard place. One, the idealist, will never move anything but has the sense of direction. The other, the pragmatist, will move plenty but has no sense of direction so it will mainly be in circles. Let us turn our attention to a possible way out of this conundrum.

The practice of pragmatic idealism

The answer lies in a philosophical stance first attributed to John Dewey at the start of the previous century: pragmatic idealism. Well, duh. Was that obvious? It is just as obvious as it is rare in my experience. Pragmatic idealism is a term often used in international policy, but is smart city technology governance not often similar to just that? It posits that it is imperative to implement ideals of virtue (think perfect TOGAF governance and templates for any and all possible architectural artifact), but also that it is wrong to discard these ideals and compromise at times in the name of expediency.

What does this mean in practice? Here are a number of principles to help you live by the ideals of pragmatic idealism (if that makes sense).

Have ideals and communicate them frequently – If we become too pragmatic, we lose the direction. We have to remember that the direction has to be set, and we need everyone to know about it, even if it is not immediately clear how we will get there. We need to provide input on whether we should go all in on open source or whether Microsoft or Amazon is a preferred vendor. Here one caveat is that we have to be very sure about the ideal, because if we first have started to communicate it, there is no way back. You will lose all credibility as a visionary if you stand up one day and say open source is the way forward and the next you sign a universal license agreement with Oracle.

This means that you have to bring a very good knowledge of where your organization is and where it wants to go. Without a solid understanding of both, you are better off playing it safe and going with the flow. That said it should quickly be possible to pick up one or two key ideals.

Ideals are expressed as architecture principles. A good format is the TOGAF formula of Name, Statement, Rationale, and Implications:

- **Name** – Should be easy to remember and represent the essence of the rule.

- **Statement** – Should clearly and precisely state the rule. It should also be nontrivial ("don't be evil" does not pass the test).

- **Rationale** – Provides a reason for the rule and highlights the benefits of it.

- **Implications** – Spells out the real-world consequences of this principle.

The first thing to do then is to flesh out these ideals and create a process through which you can create buy-in to them. Chances are that the organization already has some that you can work from, but make sure that they also align with what you feel they should be going forward.

It is also important not to have too many principles. We are shooting for something around the "magical number 7 plus or minus 2" as the title of psychologist George Miller's groundbreaking article had it. In this article, Miller demonstrated that the number of different items of information optimal for being remembered was 7 plus or minus 2. While later research has shown that it is probably even lower, this is still a good rule of thumb. Ideally you would want to be able to remember it yourself, but you also want everyone else to remember your principles as well.

Approach every problem with the minimum amount of energy and structure necessary – Wait. What? Should we be lazy? Not quite. There is actually hard science behind this. We know from the second law of thermodynamics that disorder is the only thing in the universe that comes for free and automatically. Conversely, order requires energy. Any person or organization only has a limited amount of energy. What this means is that the net effect of your architecture endeavors will be maximized with the minimum amount of order necessary. Consequently, the more thoughtfully you can use that energy, the more effective you will be.

In practical terms, this means that you should not develop 25 item templates for 9 different types of meeting minutes if you are the sole architect in a 9-man startup. You are clearly spending too much energy on creating order where it is not needed. It may be your ideal to have a template for every purpose, but maybe it can wait until the need arises. Similarly, you should not do all your architectural documentation in half sentences in your code if you are building an application with 100 million lines of code – even if your ideal is Lightweight Architecture Decision Records like the technology consultancy ThoughtWorks advocates. This is clearly too little order as no one will be able to understand or access the documentation properly.

Every problem is different. The architectural skill you have to develop is to find out how important it is. The more important a problem is, the more structure and energy it deserves. This is why documentation is higher in regulated industries like pharma and banking; it is simply a necessity to stay in business that you know why you decided to put that molecule into that drug or why a couple of hundred million dollars were transferred to the Cayman Islands. Cities have some areas that are heavily regulated and others that are not. It may therefore differ according to use case what is important.

There are different ways to gauge importance. First of all, if something is recurring frequently, chances are that it is important. At least from the perspective of efficiency, it is worthwhile to bring structure to frequently recurring events. This is why many people took the time to structure an email signature with their name and phone number. That way they do not have to write it every time someone needs it. Second, important stuff is tied to the business model. If you are in banking, data management, access control, and auditing are important. In this case, you might want to bring as much structure and predictability to that as possible. For a city, the basic utilities are high on the list like water, energy, garbage disposal, as well as public safety and health and human services. On top of this, there will be varying areas of political focus. Again, remember, if it is important, it may be worthwhile to impose structure; if it is not important, it is better to leave it simple and ad hoc.

Make every compromise count – As we saw previously, you have to make sure that the ideals you are following are known. That does not mean you can't compromise. Indeed, it is important for pragmatic idealism to compromise, but every compromise you make should be registered as such by the people on the ground. If no one knows the direction and that this is not a step in that direction, then we are just back to basic pragmatism where everything is just another step in a random direction. You have to make sure that every compromise somehow leads to a larger goal.

If you want to move to a cloud-first strategy and a given project has reservations about the cloud and wants to implement the solution in the on-premise data center, don't just say okay, even if you think it is okay for this project. Make sure that you make clear what the advantages are and agree on nontrivial reasons why this particular project does not have to go to the preferred cloud provider. Sometimes a compromise can also be used as leverage for other architectural decisions, since people know you are there to implement ideals. This can even work doubly to your advantage in that you are seen to be pragmatic and possible to work with and they will feel like they owe you or at least be on friendly terms. But beware, because it may just as well be perceived as weakness if there isn't a good reason for the compromise.

The world is divided into idealists in ivory towers watching and directing and pragmatists scurrying about in their trenches as rats in mazes, but only the pragmatic idealists can effect real change toward smarter cities. If we lean toward one, we should try to be aware of the merits of the other. Above we have considered a few principles that can be helpful:

- Have ideals and communicate them.

- Approach every problem with the minimum amount of energy and structure.

- Make every compromise count.

In order to effect change we need to think about building the right team. This is not just related to recruiting talented people but even more about getting the right mix of types on board. In the following we will look at how to select the optimal team.

Assemble the right team

Principles and the work of the architect will not do it alone. People are different and implementing innovative new solutions depends on a team. This places particular demands on choosing the right mix of personalities in the team. Employing pragmatic idealism means that you have to mix the team to support that.

The pragmatic idealist grid

In order to see more clearly the different personality profiles, we have to break down pragmatic idealism on a grid of two dimensions. The horizontal dimension signifies orientation and goes from reality to potential. This dimension is about what the person is interested in and focused on. Is the person more interested in the details of the real world and how they can be measured and manipulated or the potentials and possibilities? The vertical axis goes from contemplation to action. This has more to do with how the person relates to the world. Does he or she want to engage and do something that effects measurable change in the real world or be more retracted and think about hypotheticals whether or not they will ever be realized?

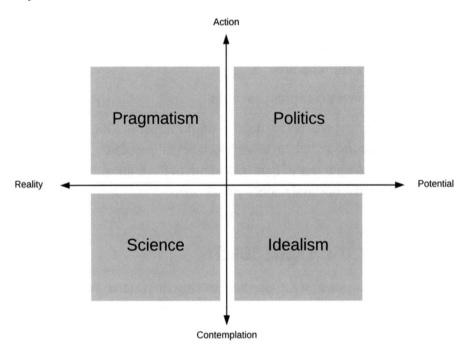

Figure 11-1. *Pragmatic idealist grid*

As we can see from the grid, four quadrants can be distinguished (see Figure 11-1). Pragmatism is characterized by a view on acting in the real world based on what is observable and tangible and what can be done about the world. The Politics quadrant is similarly concerned with acting in the real world but does it on the basis of potentialities for how the world should be. Idealism is concerned with potentials but does not have a focus on acting it out in the real world; rather, it is given to contemplation to ideas about how the world could be. Science is concerned with contemplating the real world measuring and understanding it and is not concerned with potentialities; rather, it is focused on how the world is.

Different types of person for the pragmatic idealist team

Preferably a pragmatic idealist team will not be skewed significantly toward either of these quadrants but have representation from all. This can be done by mixing the right types of people. People will exhibit different values and fall inside these different quadrants. A couple of different types can be distinguished.

Specialist – The specialist is highly skilled in execution in his area. It is someone that knows every detail of his field of operation. He has an ability to get things done even in the face of difficulties and pays little attention to why it needs to be done or whether it fits some larger scheme of good or evil. It is precisely this ability to focus on reality rather than potential that makes him valuable. Real-world examples are often athletes like Zlatan Ibrahimovic, Floyd Mayweather, or Aaron Rodgers.

In technology, it is often an external consultant who is hired precisely because of his deep expertise in a certain area. It can also be someone with a long experience in a particular area, the type where you call the system by his name, for example, John's system. This is the type of person you need to engage when you know what to get done, but not before since he is not the one to build any type of plan outside an execution plan. He will, however, often be a good source of factual information.

Tactician – The tactician continuously thinks about ways to achieve his goals through observation and experimentation. He continuously tries to find better ways to get things done within his domain. His focus is understanding how and why things work and uses this to improve the solution and processes. He needs to be at arm's length of operational work in order for it not to interfere. On the other hand, he also needs to be within reach and connected to where work takes place. His focus is not a particular solution or job at hand but a domain. They are driven by this and not larger ideas about how the world should be. Notable real-world examples are coaches like Alex Ferguson or Bill Belichick.

Many startup CEOs belong to this type, and we also find them as middle managers in larger organizations where they have acquired a good deal of operational and domain knowledge. This is a good type to engage as a bridge between someone with the ideals and visions and the team that will execute. Pair this type with a philosopher to create a pragmatic idealist core.

Revolutionary – The revolutionary is a visionary who has his eyes firmly fixed on how the world should be. He cannot be bothered by facts or information about how things are today since they need to change anyway. He typically has detailed plans for how things should be and is capable of effecting that change. On the other hand, he has very little interest in how things get done to implement his plan as long as it does.

Real-world examples include Fidel Castro, Gandhi, and Joseph Stalin. In technology, we see people like Julian Assange, Elon Musk, and in particular Steve Jobs who was famous for being able to bend reality to his view.

The archetypal revolutionary is the turnaround CEO who comes in with a lot of ideas about how things should be and little interest or time to understand how they are. In general, this type is often in a senior management position. We want to make sure to mix this type with someone who has an interest and knowledge of the real world like the engineer or the scientist.

Philosopher – The philosopher is focused on potential and understanding. He is motivated purely by contemplating how things could be with little regard to whether the ideas are being implemented or not. It is not that he does not care, quite the contrary, it is just that he does not see it as his lot to do anything about it. This is also why he is often working on ideas far into the future that can seem very vague to personalities in the pragmatic quadrant. These are ideas that have to be shaped by someone else.

In the real world, this type is often also philosophers like Karl Marx or Noam Chomsky. They all model an ideal and potential of the world that others pick up and implement. Other examples are found among nonfiction authors like Malcolm Gladwell or Daniel Pink.

In technology organizations, we often find them as enterprise architects building and designing frameworks, templates, and processes or researching and building long-term plans. They will often be the type to be tasked with developing a new strategy. Engage them in early phases to build a vision and gradually phase them out as the focus shifts to execution.

General – The general is focused on how to obtain a long-term objective, which is typically set by someone other than himself. He will be focused on understanding trends in the environment and positions of adversaries whether internal or external to the organization. He has a clear idea about where to go and is looking for repeatable processes and how to organize people and resources as well as finding the right people to execute the plan in order to move to the ideal state. He is above individual occurrences and is great at weathering a storm such as market losses. Contrary to the tactician, he is not too affected by a lost battle because he is motivated to win the war.

In real life, this is the CEO. The board sets the goals and the CEO finds a way to fulfill them. A famous real-world example is Jack Welch, but the general is also found in other types of organizations like Christine Lagarde of the ECB.

We typically find generals as senior executives, CIOs, or leaders of semi-autonomous divisions (read organizational silos). They will be commissioners or mayors in a city context because this job requires you to move through multiple repeated battles over a longer period of time toward a goal.

The general is a focal point that long-term change revolves around and needs to own the vision whether or not it was defined by him. He is visible out in front to external stakeholders and also makes his presence felt internally.

Politician – The politician is usually moving behind the scenes to effect change. He is often guided by ideals or larger goals, but they are rarely developed by himself. The actual execution however is not in his hands, and any real-world change will have to come through others. Whereas the general can delegate this, the politician works more indirectly and builds boundaries for actions through policies and agreements. These however can have a much larger and enduring impact on the world. The politician is a natural when it comes to building alliances and consensus through meetings, forums, friendships, and similar. He has a good knowledge of the positions of different people with power that he uses to engineer the expected result.

Examples from the real world are Dick Cheney who had an enormous impact on American politics without being the president. Similar people can be found in many organizations, but because they primarily work behind the scenes, they are not well known.

We see politicians as middle managers and senior managers in organizations. They sometimes have their own agenda that they can drive through sequences of different executive leadership.

This is the type of person to get involved in more complex organizations such as larger cities especially if the change horizon is longer than a few years. This person will often provide the visions for the general.

Engineer – The engineer is someone who can design a solution in detail for others to build. He is usually very specialized on a particular area of operation that requires deep insight. In order to understand this type, you have to think about a typical civil engineer who is given the task to design a bridge. He does not need to know or be interested in any way about why or what the potential of the bridge is, nor does he need to plan or carry out the actual work. He needs to find a way to do something very specific and nontrivial based on his knowledge of technology and environment.

208

A prime example is Steve Wozniak who designed the Apple I and II according to the vision of Steve Jobs. Not a lot of people of this type are well known in public because they usually do their job without any great publicity or acclaim.

Engineer types are often lead developers or solution architects with responsibility for a technical product or solution. They are frequently found as presales engineers of vendors.

The engineer needs to be engaged later in the change process when visions and masterplans have been developed. They will work well with a tactician to guide them and themselves guiding specialists.

Scientist – The scientist is a fairly well-known type frequently isolated from any expectation of real-world applicability. Still however, they are motivated to understand the real world. They see it as their duty to investigate the world. The research is often fueled by areas of interest to the surrounding world but is not applied science done to achieve an already known and expected output. He will often have very deep knowledge in a certain area and method for gaining knowledge. The deeper motivation of the scientist is to gain foundational knowledge that is new to the world. This is also what he brings to any team: a firm grounding in reality.

A good example of a famous scientist is Stephen Hawking, who investigated black holes that are of little direct practical relevance. The same can be said of Charles Darwin who also worked on problems that at the time had little practical relevance.

This type is fairly rare but can be found in an R&D division of a product-oriented company. However, it has recently resurfaced in the form of the data scientist. While they often work on more applied science type of problems, they also occasionally supply real scientific results based on their own research agenda. This can be seen in larger tech companies. For cities it is rare to have scientists employed, but they can frequently be supplied by a close-by university system.

A scientist should not make any execution plans but supply information and thought for forming the vision. He is good to pair with the revolutionary if they can be made to talk to each other. Otherwise, the tactician and the general will be able to benefit.

Tinkerer – The tinkerer is someone who tries out new stuff just for fun with little theoretical or philosophical impetus. He is motivated to understand how things work and what you can make them do. For the tinkerer, the real-world applicability and scalability is something absolutely secondary. Making something work is a goal in itself. He will usually bring a great curiosity and be on top of all the latest developments that are out there. Little or no attention will be given to scalability, maintainability, or even security of the solution since the functional potential is the focus. That said, their work is often inspired by daily experiences.

The archetypal tinkerer is Nikola Tesla who built all sorts of devices and machinery to harness the power of electricity. Many software engineers are tinkerers in their spare time and try out new technologies to get a feeling for them.

It is rare that tinkerers are employed as such. Often software engineers and infrastructure and operations people have tendencies in this direction, but most jobs have concrete expectations that are not consistent with trying out stuff for fun.

The tinkerer should be used to make practical experiments, POCs, to gain practical knowledge about a certain area. They can be combined with the tactician who has a good view for experiments that can prove effectful.

Artist – The artist is someone who is firmly fixed in the world of fiction. The essence of art is that it is not practically useful for anything. This means that the artist is completely removed from the concerns of most others in the tech industry and city government. The artist type can be a writer, typically a science fiction writer. While this is not something you would usually consider in a smart city context, science fiction is effectively driving much innovation since many working in technology are reading and watching science fiction. In this way, ideas that are far removed from the real world are used as inspiration. The artist will typically be independent and an outsider.

A real-world example is William Gibson who inspired the cyberpunk movement and numerous innovations. For example, in *Neuromancer* Gibson famously imagined the Internet years before it was created.

You will see the occasional artist as part of a think tank or conference or similar short-lived engagement, but they are rarely directly engaged in smart cities work. Rather their influence is indirect but not less forceful, since they drive the imagination that fuels real-world innovation.

The artist could be used to provide an extra touch of imagination in the very early faces of any initiative or even to define possible initiatives.

On Figure 11-2 we see the different personality types on the pragmatist idealist grid. Remember that these are ideal types and actual instances of these may not fit the grid. It should also be noted that this is not an exact science, so it can be argued that some types should have a slightly different position. However, the purpose is to reflect on the types of people to include in a team.

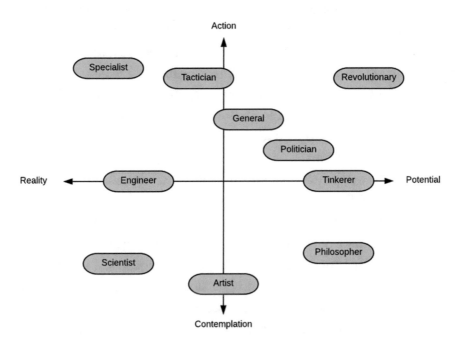

Figure 11-2. *Personality types on the pragmatic idealist grid*

Considerations in team formation

While there is no final recommendation for how to assemble a team based on the personality types, there are a few observations to be offered.

For example, if you want to drive through a smart city innovation agenda and you assemble a team of engineer types and a specialist-type project manager, don't expect them to bring about any lasting change. If they don't burn out with frustration that no one is telling them what is expected from them, they will probably make some Frankenstein type of contraptions that will appear scary to most normal people but have its own logic to them. Think something along the lines of a surveillance system installed in all city vehicles to gauge drivers's mood in real time. It's technologically impressive and nontrivial but clearly devoid of any vision or larger goal.

Vice versa, if you want to speed up smart city innovation and staff the team with revolutionaries and philosophers, don't expect much to happen either. The revolutionaries will agitate and probably get stories into the media, while the philosophers will supply the ideas and reasoning, but there is no one in the team motivated to bring this into reality.

If you want to create lasting change, you need to balance and bring in types like the politician or the general who are motivated for the long run. They need to be supplied with operational capacities like specialists, engineers, and tacticians.

If you just want to understand and build a strategy around smart cities, scientists and philosophers are great, but engineers would not necessarily thrive since the deliverable has little to do with something concrete. So it's better to leave them out in the periphery while working on the strategy.

If you want to experiment and build proof of concepts or just get a feeling for all the new and interesting possibilities that vendors bring, then the tinkerer type is what you should focus on. This is great for a context where you want to just make a lab. If you add a tactician to this team, you might end up with experiments that could prove useful in the real world too. The engineer might grow frustrated with the lack of guidance and real-world applicability.

The artist type is great for inspiration in a context where you want to build something completely new that is designed to bring attention, but don't expect multiyear executable plans.

In general, it is necessary to think about what type of smart city engagement you are looking to achieve and then cast the types to fit it. All of these types can nominally be experts in smart city technology, but if their personality type does not match the expectations, it will result in failure.

CHAPTER 12

Epilogue

Human civilization is inextricably tied to the development of cities. Cities in turn have evolved through a symbiotic relationship with technology: technology facilitated the building of ever larger cities that in turn facilitated the development of ever more sophisticated technologies. Seen in this light, smart cities are just a logical continuation of processes that have taken place for the past 5,000 to 10,000 years.

While city dwelling had been a fringe phenomenon for the majority of human history in the last 50 years, we have crossed a tipping point where the number of people living in cities has surpassed the number of those not living in cities. This development is expected to continue in the foreseeable future. This is why it is paramount that we develop a proper understanding of what smart city technology is and how we can use it optimally in the service of mankind as a continued force of civilization.

Much of smart city development has followed an unsystematic approach of ad hoc implementations similar to what Le Corbusier called the way of the pack donkey: "the pack-donkey meanders along, meditates a little in his scatter brained and distracted fashion, he zigzags in order to avoid larger stones, or to ease the climb, or to gain shade; he takes the line of least resistance." Most contemporary smart city implementations are just like that, developed for a particular need following the path of least resistance.

Rather than following the way of the pack donkey, Le Corbusier advertised the way of man, guided by logic, best exemplified by Versailles built from the ground up by Louis XIV in contrast to the

© Anders Lisdorf 2020
A. Lisdorf, *Demystifying Smart Cities*, https://doi.org/10.1007/978-1-4842-5377-9_12

pack donkey–designed Paris. Some of the most advertised smart city implementations have followed this pattern, but they often end up as artificial ghost towns, more advertising exhibits and props than stages for lived life.

Rather than being caught in this dichotomy, we should look for a third way, one in which technology gets woven into the fabric of the existing pulsating city life. Most cities are already here and will remain, so the true challenge is not whether we can build a shiny castle and lure people out to live in it, but whether we can transform the cities of today into beaming beacons of civilization that create opportunity, safety, and happiness for all the cities' residents.

We have to use our imagination to create visions of the city of tomorrow, but also find a way to merge those visions with reality in a continuous process that respects what exists and the lives and hopes of residents while daring to create transformative changes.

As this book has shown, we can do this by starting with connectivity and devices since they form the basis of the fabric of the smart city. Data is the fuel that drives solutions and must be harnessed with a focus on value and managed in a structured way similar to how oil is processed in a refinery. Applying an additional layer of artificial intelligence is crucial to go to the next level of development and harvest additional benefits, but needs to respect the humans, which technology serves. In order for anything to happen, cities need to understand and develop their ability to engage with different stakeholders to effect technological change. We have to find a way to architect with imagination and stimulate innovation. Implementing smart city solutions needs a pragmatic idealist approach where ideas and visions are developed but implemented according to the reality on the ground.

But how could the cities of tomorrow look?

Food – Since the dawn of urbanization, agriculture has been a precondition for sustaining cities of any size. The existence of a city with all its diversified professions necessitates that someone else is producing the food. Agricultural production depends on technology and tools and therefore the city. These have developed together always. But the cities of tomorrow should gradually take over food production themselves. Agricultural land is already being intensively used in a way that may not be sustainable, so we need smarter ways to produce food. Today we see rooftop gardens in some cities, but we might expand on this idea and also increase the use of vertical gardens, which will also help clean the air and give a more pleasant ambience of the city. Hydroponic farms are already now being built out and could produce a significant amount of fresh produce close to the people of the city that need it and thereby minimizing the need for transportation. Imagine that every building had its own hydroponic farm operated by robots that harvested and prepared salads for its inhabitants to purchase in a vending machine at the bottom on their way out for lunch or on their way home for dinner. All the water for irrigation would be recycled from that used by residents of the building and fertilizer would come from composting.

Energy – Already today cities are a driving force in the move toward more sustainable use of energy as the example of major US cities signing the Paris Agreement in spite of the country not entering into it. Companies like IKEA have long invested in sustainable energy and are by now energy neutral. Cities are the major consumer of energy, so continuing the path toward supplying their own energy is a logical one. Building solar panels into all surfaces could be a step in that direction; material that aesthetically look beautiful but were actually solar panels could cover the walls and power buildings. It could even produce electricity that would be stored in batteries or put out on the grid according to the needs of other consumers. Capturing excess heat from buildings and heat-generating processes like cooking, manufacturing, and all types of computing is possible today but could be expanded. In windy areas, windmills may support additional power, and wave energy from water could be a similar solution in areas close to water. Imagine living in a building block that is energy neutral like Ikea or even producing additional energy that reduces the rent of its tenants.

Mobility – Getting around has always been a major issue in a city. Today under the name of Mobility as a Service, it is one of the areas that are seeing most attention, but the mobility mix is still a major challenge as solutions are not sufficiently mature or coherent. We have to step back and think about mobility from the human view. The residents don't want to own a car or take the bus or subway in itself. They want to get from point A to point B as easily and cheaply as possible when they need to. This is the key to the mobility problem and the only thing we need to focus on. The next step is to think about how that can be done. Most attention has been given to different modes of transportation, which is part of it. But has anyone stopped to think: how about bringing point A to point B rather than bringing people from point A to point B? A big part of the increase in transportation needs historically has to do with zoning, where industrial and business zones are put in one end of the city and residence in another. In the ancient, medieval, and even modern city, mobility was not a problem simply because work, fun, and residence were all within close distance: point A was always right next to point B. Today much industry can be done without the modern and premodern pollution and noise. Take for example a manufacturing operation where robots could assemble machinery in the bottom floors and basement, where people don't want to live anyway because they want a view. These are electrical and need not make any noise. Electrical autonomous trucks that are similarly silent may collect finished goods and supply parts in the night when everyone is sleeping and no commuters are on the roads.

When movement is necessary, the key issue to solve is one of interoperability. How do all the excellent opportunities for transportation merge? There should be one big mobility platform where all mobility could be handled, where autonomous busses, ride hailing and taxis, scooters, busses and metros are all connected and interfaced and purchased through the same interface to provide the consumer with a coherent mobility layer where new solutions and offerings can plug in seamlessly regardless of vendor; a planetary mobility fabric that optimizes on the supply and demand sides continuously to get human kind from point A to point B in the smartest possible way.

Recycling – Since many resources that the city needs are if not scarce then finite, a gradual move toward recycling and the circular economy has to be made. The first step is to look at waste as a resource. Collecting waste could be done by autonomous trash robots and trucks that are electric and therefore silent. They can move around in the night, with smaller ones collecting garbage in parks and on streets emptying trash cans when they signal they are full. All of this is taken to sorting plants that recognize the nature of all the garbage collected and sort it into different categories depending on their reuse potential. Similarly, electronics are disassembled and reused. Some components may be reused as is, such as CPUs; others will be further processed to extract valuable components like metals and rare earths. Mining operations will start in old dump yards, where mining techniques are used to identify and develop promising sites. Human waste is recycled to natural gas and fertilizer for the city farms, and excess heat is stored in underground geothermic facilities.

All of these ideas are not far off or particularly fancy from a technical point of view. No fundamentally new technologies have to be developed to do any of those previously mentioned. What is needed is focus and political leadership. For example, in order for buildings to become food producing and energy self-sufficient, politicians need to require them to be that. In order for the industry to move closer to residence, politicians need to require it. The policy tools are already there in the shape of zoning laws, building codes, laws, and regulations. For example, why not make some of the prime real estate development sites in cities the first targets of these increased demands on energy self-sufficiency? If a developer wants to build, this is an increased cost for sure, but since these are the most valuable plots, they could be economic and drive the technology and know-how, thereby lowering the prices of implementing similar features in other buildings. In this way, politicians can start by looking at available policy tools to start a dynamic to radically more self-sufficient and sustainable cities.

Self-sustaining cities are also vital for the next frontier of human civilization: space. Within a hundred years, the first budding cities will begin to appear in our solar system – presumably the moon and Mars first, but other targets such as the moons of Jupiter and Saturn are other good candidates for future cities. These cities will not have nearby farms where you can go to buy apples or distribution centers from where you can get a new computer delivered next day through a carrier service. Virtually everything needs to be produced and recycled within the context of the city.

In the future cities in space, we have to be able to produce our own food. Not only do we need hydroponic farms but also advanced gene editing solutions. We can't bring the seeds of all the crop we want, and we can't foresee what traits are needed to be strengthened in the new surroundings. If a crop starts to fail, we can't just order another. Similarly, humans may find themselves with other nutritional needs that their crops have to supply. We cannot expect rich sources of water, so recycling that will be another key issue.

On faraway planets, the debate over fossil fuels or sustainable energy is vacuous; since there will only be sustainable energy sources in the beginning, cities have to harness solar and geothermal energy to survive. As for mobility, we will be back to a situation where everything is close; there are no ride hailing services in space, so our cities have to locate everything close by and have the potential to build a coherent transportation solution from the start. We will end up with an interplanetary transportation fabric. Recycling will similarly not be a choice but a necessity. Every chip, circuit, poop, and boot will have to enter the circular economy and be reprocessed. Waste is not an option in space.

Building smarter cities makes sense now and is good for the environment, economies, and lives of their residents today, but we might also use it as a stepping stone to prepare for the next frontier of civilization: the solar system and beyond.

References

The references in this section are meant as a help for the interested reader to find additional information and explore in more detail the subjects that are touched on in the book. Direct citations and subject matter treated directly in the text are included here. It is not in any way meant to be exhaustive of the subject nor the literature that was used for this book.

Chapter 1

Understanding Early Civilizations: A Comparative Study, Bruce G. Trigger, Cambridge University Press, 2003

State of the World's Cities 2010/2011 Bridging the Urban Divide, United Nations Human Settlement Programme, 2010

Scale: the universal laws of growth, innovation, sustainability, and the pace of life in organisms, cities, economies, and companies, Geoffrey West, Penguin, 2017

The City of To-Morrow and its planning, Le Corbusier, Dover Publications, 1987

Understanding Smart City Transformation with Best Practices, IDC White Paper, November 2017

The City of Tomorrow: Sensors, Networks, Hackers, and the future of Urban Life, Carlo Ratti and Matthew Claudel, Yale University Press, 2016

A New Digital Deal, Bas Boorsma, Rainmaking publications, 2017

Smart sustainable cities: An analysis of definitions – Focus Group Technical Report, ITU-T, October 2014

Smart Cities: Digital Solutions for a More Liveable Future, McKinsey Global Institute, June 2018

© Anders Lisdorf 2020
A. Lisdorf, *Demystifying Smart Cities*, https://doi.org/10.1007/978-1-4842-5377-9

Chapter 2

Collective Dynamics of Small-World Networks, Duncan Watts, S. Strogatz, Nature 393, 440–442 1998

https://web.archive.org/web/20140803231327/http://www.nyc.gov/html/doitt/downloads/pdf/payphone_rfi.pdf (October 2, 2019) the original RFI for what turned out to be LinkNYC from 2012

www1.nyc.gov/office-of-the-mayor/news/923-14/de-blasio-administration-winner-competition-replace-payphones-five-borough (October 2, 2019) press release of the winner of the LinkNYC bid

www.citylab.com/life/2015/04/de-blasios-vision-for-new-york-broadband-for-all-by-2025/391092/ (October 2, 2019) an article about Mayor of New York Bill De Blasio's plan for broadband for all in New York by 2025

www1.nyc.gov/site/doitt/agencies/nycwin.page (October 2, 2019) a description of The New York City Wireless Network, known as NYCWiN

www.thethingsnetwork.org (October 5, 2019) a project dedicated to building LoRaWAN solutions

Chapter 3

https://dyn.com/blog/dyn-analysis-summary-of-friday-october-21-attack/ (October 2, 2019) the official analysis of the Dyn attack on October 21

https://citiesfordigitalrights.org (October 2, 2019) the official site for the Cities for Digital Rights coalition

www.theguardian.com/world/2018/jan/28/fitness-tracking-app-gives-away-location-of-secret-us-army-bases (October 2, 2019) an article about the Strava fitness tracking incident involving a US Army base

https://en.wikipedia.org/wiki/Stuxnet (October 2, 2019) a description from Wikipedia of the Stuxnet worm `https://nvlpubs.nist.gov/nistpubs/FIPS/NIST.FIPS.199.pdf` (October 2, 2019) the official FIPS 199 standard for categorization of information and information systems

`https://en.wikipedia.org/wiki/Federal_Information_Security_Management_Act_of_2002` (October 2, 2019) a description of the FISMA framework from Wikipedia

`https://arrayofthings.github.io/` (October 2, 2019) the official site of the Array of Things project

`http://maps.nyc.gov/snow/#` (October 2, 2019) the PlowNYC site where New Yorkers can track the progress of snow plows during wintertime

Chapter 4

`https://scijinks.gov/air-quality/`

`www.epa.gov/pm-pollution/particulate-matter-pm-basics` (October 2, 2019) definition of what particulate matter is

`https://brightplanet.com/2013/06/twitter-firehose-vs-twitter-api-whats-the-difference-and-why-should-you-care/` (October 2, 2019) a description of how the Twitter Firehose works

`www.waze.com/ccp` (October 2, 2019) official site of the Twitter Connected Citizens Program

The NIST Definition of Cloud Computing, Peter M. Mell & Timothy Grance, Special Publication (NIST SP) – 800–145

September 2011 (Updated November 2018)

Assessing the Optimal Data Stores for Modern Architectures, Sanjeev Mohan, Gartner, February 2019

A Relational Model of Data for Large Shared Data Banks, E. F. Codd, Communications of the ACM 377–387, 1970

NoSQL Distilled: A Brief Guide to the Emerging World of Polyglot Persistence, Pramod Sadalage & Martin Fowler, Addison-Wesley, 2012

REFERENCES

Data Integration – Global Market Outlook (2017–2026), Stratistics, March 2018

https://opendata.cityofnewyork.us/ (October 2, 2019) the official site of the Open Data portal of New York City

Chapter 5

https://emerj.com/ai-sector-overviews/smart-city-artificial-intelligence-applications-trends/ (October 2, 2019) an article about AI implementations in US cities

www.theverge.com/2019/4/15/18309437/new-york-city-accountability-task-force-law-algorithm-transparency-automation (October 2, 2019) an article about New York City's algorithm task force

https://legistar.council.nyc.gov/LegislationDetail.aspx?ID=3137815&GUID=437A6A6D-62E1-47E2-9C42-461253F9C6D0 (October 2, 2019) the official publication of Local Law 49 of 2018 in New York City that requires a task force to provide recommendations about automated decision systems

https://alvelor.com/ (October 2, 2019) the official site of the open source traffic camera computer vision project Alvelor

Computing Machinery and Intelligence, Alan M. Turing, Mind 49, 433–460, 1950

The Hundred-Page Machine Learning Book, Andriy Burkov, 2019

Chapter 6

Diffusion of Innovations (5th edition), Rogers, Everett M., Free Press, 2003

https://commons.wikimedia.org/wiki/File:Diffusion_of_ideas.svg (September 25, 2019) the source of Figure 6-1

Chapter 7

Yes is More: An Archicomic on Architectural Evolution, Bjarke Ingels, Taschen 2009

www.youtube.com/watch?v=cIsIKv1lFZw (September 27, 2019) a video by Bjarke Ingels: architecture should be more like Minecraft

Chapter 8

The Power of Habit: Why We Do What We Do, and How to Change, Charles Duhigg, Random House, 2013

Chapter 9

Scoring Points, How Tesco Continues to Win Customer Loyalty, Clive Humby, Terry Hunt and Tim Phillips, Kogan Page, 2008

The World's Most Valuable Resource is no longer Oil but Data, The Economist, May 6th 2017

Enterprise Integration Patterns, Gregor Hohpe and Bobby Woolf, Addison Wesley, 2003

The Data Warehouse Toolkit: The Definitive Guide to Dimensional Modelling, Ralph Kimball and Margy Ross, Wiley 2013

Hadoop: The Definitive Guide, Tom White, O'Reilly Media, 2015

Chapter 10

www.wired.com/2010/11/1110mars-climate-observer-report/
(October 2, 2019) a story about the Mars Climate Orbiter's crash

https://bleacherreport.com/articles/2760821-olympic-mens-alpine-skiing-results-2018-medal-winners-for-slalom (October 2, 2019) the results of the 2018 Olympic show a difference less than 1.5 seconds between number 1 and 10

https://home.cern/science/computing/processing-what-record (October 2, 2019) a description of what the Large Hadron Collider processes

Chapter 11

The Magical Number Seven, Plus or Minus Two Some Limits on Our Capacity for Processing Information, George A. Miller, Psychological Review Vol 101, no. 2, page 343–352, 1955

https://pubs.opengroup.org/architecture/togaf8-doc/arch/chap29.html (October 2, 2019) a description of the Open Group's format for Principles

Index

A

American National Institute of Standards and Technology (NIST), 91, 92
Architectural layers, 64
Architecture standards
    connectivity, 64
    data, 65
    devices, 64, 66
    integration, 64
    platform, 64
Array of Things (AoT), 68
Artificial intelligence (AI), 18, 216
    Alvelor project, 136
    Amsterdam 311, 136
    challenges, 107, 108
    history, 105, 106
    issues
        autonomous vehicles and ethics, 120, 122
        ecological, 123, 124
        human intelligence, 119
        optimization paradox, 126–128
        political accountability, 130
        public demand, 130
        unacceptable implementation, 131
    unclear benefits, 129
    unpredictable human element, 131
    solutions, 133–135
Availability, 60
AWS, 10, 28, 51, 53, 80

B

Better Approach To Mobile Adhoc Networking (B.A.T.M.A.N.), 35
Block chain, 83–85
Bluetooth, 25
Bus topology, 27, 29–30, 34

C

Chief Information Security Officer (CISO), 55, 56, 58
Cities coalition for digital rights, 66, 67
Cities, history and future
    civilizations, 2
    data usage, 74
    pack donkey, 4
    technology, 5
    urbanization, 2
    urbanocene period, 3

A. Lisdorf, *Demystifying Smart Cities*, https://doi.org/10.1007/978-1-4842-5377-9

Printed in the United States
By Bookmasters